The Power of God unto Salvation

Benjamin B. Warfield

Solid Ground Christian Books
PO Box 660132 ~Vestavia Hills AL 35266

SOLID GROUND CHRISTIAN BOOKS
PO Box 660132, Vestavia Hills, AL 35266
205-443-0311
sgcb@charter.net
http://www.solid-ground-books.com

The Power of God unto Salvation

by Benjamin B. Warfield (1851-1921)

From the 1930 edition by Eerdmans of Grand Rapids, MI

Published by Solid Ground Christian Books

Classic Reprints Series

First printing of hardcover edition July 2003
First printing of paperback edition October 2004

ISBN: 1-932474-09-9 (hardcover)
ISBN: 1-932474-10-2 (paperback)

Solid Ground Christian Books gratefully acknowledges Special Collections, Princeton Theological Seminary Libraries for assisting us in obtaining the materials used in the appendix.

Manufactured in the United States of America

PREFACE

B.B. Warfield (1851-1921) is best known as one of the towering geniuses in the last one hundred years of American church life. Born near Lexington, Kentucky, he graduated from both the University and the Seminary at Princeton and in 1887 returned to the Seminary as a theology professor.

Warfield wrote a number of books on a variety of subjects. After his death, Oxford University Press published a magnificent ten volume set of his articles. These, as well as several of his books, have been reprinted. More recently a further two volumes of his shorter writings have also been published. Thus, seventy years after his death, his writings are probably more widely read and appreciated than ever.

The range and penetration of Warfield's knowledge is breathtaking: he was a skilled New Testament scholar, a patient historian, a widely read theologian, and a learned controversialist. All this was married to an easy style which guaranteed that his work can be read today with pleasure.

These qualities are the fruit of living in a community of Christian scholars, as Warfield did at Princeton. Here he enjoyed many uninterrupted hours of study, reflection, and writing. But his life was not free from personal burden and inner pain. Shortly after his marriage, Warfield and his wife were caught in a thunderstorm. The severity of it had an overpowering and debilitating effect on Mrs. Warfield and left her virtually an invalid for the rest of her life. Her husband thereafter allowed his life and work to be circumscribed by her condition and rarely seems to have left her side for periods of any length. In the providence of God, however, this limitation on his movements became the plowed field in which the seed thoughts of his fertile mind grew into the harvest of scholarly articles and books he later wrote.

Warfield, however, was not *exclusively* a scholar. Indeed, for all his learning, he was not even *primarily* a scholar. He was first and foremost a Christian and a minister of the gospel. Thus, in addition to the instruction of the class, he also preached. And what material! - as will soon become obvious from this volume, which is composed of a selection his sermons first published one hundred years ago.

Of course, these sermons could only have been composed by a scholar. Yet they are not scholastic. Admittedly, they also demanded more from their hearers than the well-packaged, story-dominated sermons of our own day; but they were magnificently crafted, and full of biblical protein for the mind and heart. There is nothing eccentric in them; they exude grace. Our own efforts today seem weak, and yes, ugly, by comparison.

Nowhere is this more true than in teaching and preaching about the Gospel of Christ, —the theme of these sermons. In a day when the Gospel is muddled in the preaching and thinking of so many, Warfield here gives mature instruction, wonderful insight, and, at times, breathtakingly beautiful exposition. These are pages to ponder and treasure.

Such a recommendation is, clearly, the testimony of an enthusiast. Indeed, but only because like a multitude of others, I have come to appreciate the great gift Warfield was to the Christian Church.

I commend these pages, then, as one who has again and again been helped by their contents. Solid Ground Christian Books has put us all in its debt by publishing this fine volume of sermons that has been unavailable for nearly seventy-five years. It is a treasure to be read and enjoyed again and again. If you have never made Warfield's acquaintance before, this is an ideal place to begin. With so much of his writing still readily available, I think it is safe to predict that it will be the first of many profitable meetings.

Sinclair B. Ferguson

Westminster Theological Seminary

Dallas, Texas USA

CONTENTS

I. The Revelation of Man —*Hebrews 2:6-9* 3

II. The Saving Christ —*1 Timothy 1:15* 29

III. The Argument from Experience —*Romans 5:1,2* 57

IV. The Paradox of Omnipotence —*Mark 10:27* 93

V. The Love of the Holy Ghost —*James 5:5* 121

VI. The Leading of the Spirit —*Romans 8:14* 151

VII. Paul's Earliest Gospel —*1 Thessalonians 1:2,4; 5:9,24* . 183

VII. False Religions and the True —*Acts 17:23* 219

Appendix —*Hymns and Religious Verses by B.B. Warfield* . . 257

I

THE REVELATION OF MAN

THE
POWER OF GOD UNTO SALVATION

I

THE REVELATION OF MAN

"But one hath somewhere testified, saying, What is man, that Thou art mindful of him? Or the son of man, that Thou visitest him? Thou madest him a little lower than the angels; Thou crownedst him with glory and honor; Thou didst put all things in subjection under his feet. For in that He subjected all things unto him, He left nothing that is not subject to him. But now we see not yet all things subjected to him. But we behold Him who hath been made a little lower than the angels, even Jesus, because of the suffering of death, crowned with glory and honor."—HEB. ii. 6-9. (R. V.)

THESE words form the beginning of a marvelous passage the subject of which is "Christ our Representative." That He might become our Representative, the inspired writer teaches, it was needful that He should identify Himself with us. Therefore it was that He became man.

Language had been exhausted to exhibit the divine dignity of our Representative. In contrast with those men of God, the prophets, in whom

God dwelt and through whom God spoke, He is called a Son through whom the worlds were made and by the word of whose power all things are upheld; who is the effulgence of God's glory and the very impression of His substance. In contrast with the most exalted of the creatures of God, the angels, He is given the more excellent name of the Son of God, His firstborn, whom all the angels of God shall worship; nay, He is given the name of the almighty and righteous God Himself, of the eternal Lord, who in the beginning laid the foundations of the earth and framed the heavens, and who shall abide the same when heaven and earth wax old and pass away.

Language is now exhausted to emphasize the perfection of the identification of this divine being with the children of men, when He who by nature was thus infinitely exalted above angels was made, like man, "a little lower than the angels . . . because of the suffering of death." "It behooved Him," we are told, "in all things to be made like unto His brethren"; and "since then the children are sharers in blood and flesh, He also Himself in like manner partook of the same," in order "that through death He might bring to nought him that had the power of death, that is, the devil; and might deliver all them who through fear of death were all their lifetime subject to bondage." The emphasis is upon the completeness of the identification of the Son of God with the sons of men, that by His sufferings many sons might be brought unto glory. And the implication is that as He was thus so completely identified with us for His work, so we are equally completely identified with Him in the fruits of that work. He shared with us our estate that we might share His merit with Him.

There is a great deal more precious truth in this passage than we can profitably attempt to consider in a single discourse The whole gospel of the grace of God is in it. I have chosen its initial words for my text, and I purpose to ask you to fix your attention on its initial thought—the perfect identification of Christ with man. And even this in only one of its aspects, viz.: the consequent revelation of man which is brought us by the man Christ Jesus. Because our Lord is the Son of God, the impressed image of God's substance—as the stamp of a seal is the impressed image of the seal—His advent into our world was the supreme revelation of God. But, equally, because of His perfect identification with the children of men, partaking of their blood and flesh, and made in all things like unto men, He stands before us also as the perfect revelation of man. It behooves us to look with wondering eyes upon Him whom to see is to see the Father also, that we may learn to know God—the God and Father of our Lord Jesus Christ, who "so loved the world, that He gave His only begotten Son, that whosoever believeth on Him should not perish, but have eternal life." It may also behoove us to look upon Him who is not ashamed to call us brethren, that we may learn to know man—the man that God made in His own image, and whom He would rescue from his sin by the gift of His Son.

The text assuredly fully justifies us in looking upon Christ as the revelation of man. It begins, as you observe, by adducing the language of the eighth Psalm, in which God is adoringly praised for His goodness to man in endowing him, despite his comparative insignificance, with dominion over the creatures. The psalmist is contemplating the mighty expanse of the evening sky, studded with its orbs of light, among which the moon marches in splendor; and he is filled with a sense of the greatness of the God the work of whose hands all this glory is. "O Lord, our Lord, how excellent is Thy name in all the earth, who hast set Thy glory upon the heavens!" He is lost in wonder that such a God can bear in mind so weak a thing as man. "When I consider Thy heavens, the work of Thy fingers, the moon and the stars, which Thou hast ordained; what is man, that Thou art mindful of him, and the son of man, that Thou visitest him?" But his wonder and adoration reach their climax as he recounts how the Author of all this magnificent universe has not only considered man, but made him lord of it all. In an inextinguishable burst of amazed praise he declares: "Thou hast made him but little lower than the angels, and crownedst him with glory and honor. Thou madest him to have dominion over the works of Thy hands; Thou hast put all things under his feet." He enumerates the minor elements of man's strange dominion, emphasizing its completeness and all-inclusiveness. "All sheep and oxen, yea, and the beasts of the field; the fowl of the air, and the fish of the sea, whatsoever passeth through the paths of the seas." Nothing is omitted. So the praise returns upon itself and the Psalm closes with the repeated and now justified exclamation, "O Lord, our Lord, how excellent is Thy name in all the earth!" It is a hymn, you observe, of man's dignity and honor and dominion. God is praised that He has dealt in so wondrous a fashion with mortal man, born from men, that He has elevated him to a position but little lower than that of the angels, crowned him with glory and honor, and given him dominion over all the works of His hands.

Now, observe how the author of this epistle deals with the Psalm. He adduces it as authoritative Scripture declaring indisputable fact. "One hath somewhere testified, saying, What is man, that Thou art mindful of him? Or the son of man, that Thou visitest him? Thou madest him a little lower than the angels; Thou crownedst him with glory and honor; Thou didst put all things in subjection under his feet." He expounds its meaning accurately. "For in that He subjected all things unto him, He left nothing that is not subject to him." And then he argues thus: "But now we see not yet all things subjected to him. But we behold Him who hath been made a little lower than the angels, even Jesus, because of the suffering of death, crowned with glory and honor." That is, of course, in Jesus only as yet do we see in actual possession and exercise, in its completeness and perfection, that majesty and dominion which the

THE REVELATION OF MAN 9

inspired psalmist attributes to man. God has expressly subjected all things to man; man has obviously not entered into his dominion; but the man Jesus has. Therefore it is to Him that we are to look if we would see man as man, man in the possession and use of all those faculties, powers, dignities for which he was destined by his Creator. In this way the author of this epistle presents Jesus before us as the pattern, the ideal, the realization of man. Looking upon Him, we have man revealed to us.

I beg you to keep fully in mind that our Lord's adaptation to reveal to us what man is, is based by the author of this epistle solely on the perfection of His identification with us in His incarnation. To the author of this epistle, our Lord in His own proper person is beyond all comparison with man. As God's own Son, the effulgence of His glory and the impressed image of His substance, He is beyond comparison even with prophets and infinitely above angels. He became identified with us by an act of humiliation and for an assigned cause, viz.: for the sake "of the suffering of death," that is, in order that He might be able to undertake and properly to fulfill His high-priestly work—as we are immediately instructed in detail. This act of humiliation is expressed here, for the sake of giving point to the argument, in language derived from the Psalm: "He hath been made a little lower than the angels." Observe, then, the pregnant difference which emerges in the use of this phrase of man and of our Lord. That man was made but little lower than the angels marks the height of his exaltation: "Thou didst make him a little lower than the angels, Thou didst crown him with glory and honor." That our Lord was made a little lower than the angels, marks the depth of His humiliation: "We behold Jesus, who hath been made a little lower than the angels for the suffering of death." So wide is the interval that stretches between Him and man. He stoops to reach the exalted heights of man's as yet unattained glory.

But the perfection of His identification with us consisted just in this, that He did not, when He was made a little lower than the angels for the suffering of death, assume merely the appearance of man or even merely the position and destiny of man, but the reality of humanity. Note the stress laid in the passage, on the reality of the humanity which our Lord assumed, when, as the inspired writer pointedly declares, He was made like to His brethren in all things. He was made like them in their physical nature: as they were "sharers in blood and flesh, He also Himself in like manner partook of the same." He was made like them in their psychical nature: as they suffered and were tempted, He also "Himself hath suffered being tempted." Jesus Christ is presented before us here as a true and real man, possessed of every faculty and capacity that belongs to the essence of our nature: as a veritable "son of man," born of a woman, and brother to all those whom He came to succor. It is because He was in this true and complete sense what He so loved to call Himself, the Son of man—doubtless with as full reference to the eighth Psalm as to Daniel's great apocalypse—that He reveals to us in His own life and conduct what man was intended to be in the plan of God.

We must keep these great facts in mind that we may preserve the point of view of the inspired writer, as we strive to follow him in looking upon Jesus as the representative man, in whose humanity man is revealed to us. He is not the representative man in the sense that man is all that He is. When He entered the sphere of human life, by the assumption of a human nature,

He did not lay aside His Godhead. He is, while being all that man is, infinitely more. He is God as well as man. He is not the representative man in the sense that in Him the age-long process of man's creation was first completed—that His exalted humanity is the goal toward which nature had been all through the aeons travailing, till now at last in Him the man-child comes to a tardy birth. He is the revelation of man only in the sense that when we turn our eyes toward Him, we see in the quality of His humanity God's ideal of man, the Creator's intention for His creature; while by contrast with Him we may learn the degradation of our sin; and happily also we may see in Him what man is to be, through the redemption of the Son of God and the sanctification of the Spirit. Let us think a little on these things.

And, first, in the quality of Christ's manhood we may see the perfect man, the revelation of what man is in God's idea of him, of what the Creator intended him to be.

And what is the quality of Jesus' manhood? There is no other word to express it except the great word perfection. Sin? We cannot think of it in connection with Him. Those who companied with Him testify that He was "without blemish and without spot"; that "He did no sin, neither was guile found in His mouth." The author of our epistle declares that He was "separate from sinners," that He was, in the midst of temptation, "without sin." The story of His life and sayings leaves us without trace of acknowledgment of fault on His own part, without betrayal of consciousness of unworthiness, without the slightest hint of inner conflict with sinful impulses.

And if the quality of His excellence is too positive to permit us even to speak of sin in connection with it, it is equally too universal to admit of adequate characterization. The excellences of the best of men may usually be condensed in a single outstanding virtue or grace by which each is peculiarly marked. Thus we speak of the faith of Abraham, the meekness of Moses, the patience of Job, the boldness of Elijah, the love of John. The perfection of Jesus defies such particularizing characterization. All the beauties of character which exhibit themselves singly in the world's saints and heroes, assemble in Him, each in its perfection and all in perfect balance and harmonious combination. If we ask what manner of man He was, we can only respond, No manner of man, but rather, by way of eminence, *the* man, the only perfect man that ever existed on earth, to whom gathered all the perfections proper to man and possible for man, that they might find a fitting home in His heart and that they might play brightly about His person. If you would know what man is, in the height of His divine idea, look at Jesus Christ.

Is it not well for the world once to have seen such a man? How easy it is to accuse nature of our faults, to confront God with what we have wrought, and to seek to roll upon our Creator the responsibility for the creatures which our own deeds have made us. How easy to look upon corruption as the inevitable incident of existence for such beings as men; and to speak of sin as only the mark of our humanity. How easily a cynical temper waxes within us as we mix with men in the world's marts and tread with them the devious paths of life. We mark their ways and ask, waiting, like Pilate, for no answer, Who shall show us any good? How easily our ideals themselves sink to what we fancy the level of human powers. We note the aims of those who strive about us. We note the aims of the great figures which flit across the pages of history, commanding the acclamation of all the ages. We look within at the seething caldron of passions and impulses of our own souls. Do not all these voices call us to one natural, one unavoidable issue? If in the far distance we faintly discover hanging above us the beckoning glimmer of some star of heaven—what is poor wingless man, that he should hope to rise to grasp it? Is it not the part of wisdom, as well as the demand of nature, that worms shall crawl? Is it not folly unspeakable for such as we to attempt to mount the skies? But we see Jesus, and the scales fall from our eyes; in Him we perceive what man is in his idea, and what it may be well for him to seek to become.

The man Jesus stands before us as the revelation of man's native dignity, capacities, and powers. He exhibits to us what man is in the idea of his Maker. He uncovers to our view, in their perfection and strength, those qualities and forces of good, the ruins of which only we may see in our fellow-men, and enables us to admire, honor, love, and hope for them, because they still possess such qualities and capacities though in ruins. To look upon Him is to ennoble and elevate our ideals of life; the sight of Him forbids us to forget our higher nature and higher aspirations; it quickens in us our dead longings to be like Him, men after God's plan and heart, rather than after our own corrupt impulses. It is well for the world once to have seen such a man.

Once and once only. Ah, there is the pity of it, and there is the despair of it! In no other than in Him has the ideal ever been realized. And the more we look upon His perfections the more we perceive, as in no other light, how far short of the ideal man have been our highest imaginations. For we need to note, secondly, that in the light of Jesus' perfect manhood we have, by contrast, revealed to us what man is in his sin and depravity, what he has made himself in his rebellion from good and from God.

The Greeks had a proverb: "By the straight is judged both the straight and the crooked; the rule is singly the test of both." And so it is. Wherever the straight is brought to light, there inevitably is also the crookedness of the crooked made visible. Let the builder hang his plumbline, with whatever careless intent, over any wall; and if the wall be not straight, every wayfarer may perceive it. Let the carpenter lay his straightedge alongside of any board, and every crook and bend is brought to the instant observation of all.

This is what is meant when the Scriptures tell us that by the law is the knowledge of sin. For the law is for moral things what the plumb-line and the straight-edge are for physical things: it is the rule by which our hearts are measured and in the presence of which what we really are is made manifest. We may sin and scarcely know we sin, until the straight-edge of the law is brought against us. Oh, how we fall away from its line of rectitude!

Now, our blessed Saviour, as the perfect one, full of righteousness and holiness, is the embodiment of the law in life. And more perfectly and vividly than any law—though that law be holy and just and good—does His presence among men measure men and reveal what men are. The presence of any good man in our midst acts, in its due proportion, as such a measure. And, therefore, from the beginning of the world men have been stung by the presence of a good man among them to hatred of him, and have evilly entreated and persecuted him. He is a standing accusation of their sins. "There is certainly," says Miss Yonge in *The Heir of Redcliffe* —that uplifting story which has been such a factor in the lives of such men as Mr. William Morris and Dr. A. Kuyper—" there is certainly a 'tyrannous hate' in the world for unusual goodness, which is a rebuke to it." But no man ever so feels his utter depravity as when he thinks of himself as standing by the side of Jesus. In this presence, even what we had fondly looked upon as our virtues hide their faces in shame and cry, Depart from us, for we are sinful in thy sight, O Lord.

Lay open the narrative in these gospels, of how the Son of man went about among men, in the days of His sojourn here below. Note on the one hand the ever-growing glory of that revelation of a perfect life. And note on the other hand the ever-increasing horror of the accompanying revelation of human weakness and human depravity. It could not be otherwise. When we see Jesus, it must be in the brightness of His unapproachable splendor that we see those about Him: as it is in the light of the sun that we see the forms and colors and characters of all objects on which it turns its beams. Especially when we see Him in conflict with His enemies, as we cannot avoid being moved with amazement by the spectacle of His utter perfection; so must we, in that light, be shocked by the spectacle of the utter depravity of men. Men are revealed in this presence in their true, their fundamental tones of nature with a vivid completeness in which they are never seen elsewhere.

Now, such a crisis as this, Jesus is bringing into the life of every man upon whom the light of His knowledge shines. No man can escape the test. Christ Jesus has come into the world and He confronts every one with the spectacle of His perfect humanity. When men are least thinking of Him, lo! there He is by their side. Every time His name is mentioned in the assemblies of men, every time His image rises in a brooding human heart, the crisis comes again to human souls. They may not realize it; they may prefer otherwise; they may determine otherwise. But they are being tried and tested against their wills every moment they live in His presence. Some, like the priests, burn with rage at every thought of the supreme claim He makes upon their homage, and refuse with all violence to have this man to rule over them. Others, like Pilate, yield a languid and chill recognition to His goodness and worth, yet choose the pursuit of pleasure or gain above the service of Him. Others, like the mob, may in easy indifference prefer some other leader, though he be a robber and a murderer. Thus a crisis is brought by His presence to every heart; and a revelation of man in his true depravity is the result. As He moves through the world the whole race lies at His feet self-condemned. We shudder as, in the light of His brightness, we see man as he is.

Yet we have the word of Jesus Himself for it that God sent not His Son into the world to condemn the world, but that the world through Him might be saved. Let us turn our eyes away, then, from the terrible spectacle of a race revealed in its sin to observe, in the third place, that in the perfection of Christ's manhood we have the revelation of what man may become by the redemption of the Son of God and the sanctification of the Spirit.

We observe that the element of promise is made very prominent in the text and in the wider passage of which the text is a part. Mark those words of hope, "Not yet." "We see not yet all things subjected to him." The psalmist's ascription is then yet to be fulfilled in man himself. In Jesus' dominion, and in Jesus' perfection, we are to see only the earnest and the pledge. When He entered through sufferings into glory, it was in the process of bringing many sons unto glory. If He is the sanctifier, they are the sanctified; and He is not ashamed to call them brethren. If He became like them in order that He might die in their behalf; this death was to be accomplished in order that He might, by making propitiation for their sins, deliver them from their bondage. In a word, we are to look upon Jesus in His perfect manhood as our forerunner. In His perfection we are to see the revelation of what we too shall be when He shall have perfected His work in us as He has already perfected it for us.

Let us bless God for these precious assurances. Without them the sight of Jesus could but bring us despair. Men speak of Him, indeed, as our example; and we praise God that He has given us such an example—we bless His holy name that He has permitted the world to see one such man. But if He were only our example, as we looked upon Him and saw His perfection and by contrast saw our depravity, who would not cry that this example is too high, we cannot attain unto it!

I fear we do not always consider with what limitations mere example is hedged about. Limitations of space. How narrow a circle can really feel the uplift of even the most moving personal example. At the best, only those who cluster most nearly round the figure of a good man, however impressive, can be much affected by his example. Limitations of time. How soon the force of the mightiest personality is drowned in the stream of the years. As the flood of days falls over it how rapidly it becomes at best a story —an empty name. Could Jesus have declared that it was expedient for Him to go away, if it were only or chiefly as an example that He came into the world? Would not it have been rather expedient that He should have lived through all the ages, and kept His living example as a living force before the eyes of men for all time and in every land? Limitations of power. The most inspiring example cannot change the heart, cannot impart new life to a dead soul. At best it can but deflect the direction of powers already existent and operative. We thank God that Christ is our example, that we see in Him all that we fain would be. But we thank Him that He is much more than our example; that He is our life as well. It is only because He is our life, that as our example He can be our hope and joy.

With Him as only our example we could see in His perfect manhood only what we ought to be, ought but cannot. Hopeless gloom would inevitably settle upon our souls. With Him as our life, who has died for our sins and purchased the sanctifying Spirit for us, we see in His perfect manhood what we are to be. Do we peer into that mysterious future, with doubt if not dismay? We have the precious assurance based upon His perfected work of propitiation and purchase: "Beloved, now are we children of God, and it is not yet made manifest what we shall be. We know that, if He shall be manifested, we shall be like Him." "We shall be like Him." Our hearts take courage, and we rest on this word. We shall be like Him! "We all remember," says Bishop Gore, "the pathetic words of Simmias in the argument with Socrates about the immortality of the soul. 'I dare say,' he says, 'that you, Socrates, feel as I do, how very hard and almost impossible is the attainment of any certainty about questions such as these in the present life. And yet I should deem him a coward who did not prove what is said about them to the uttermost, or whose heart failed him before he had examined them on every side. For he should persevere until he has ascertained one of two things: either he should discover and learn the truth about them; or, if this is impossible, I would have him take the best and most irrefragable of human notions, and let this be the raft on which he sails through life—not without risk, as I admit, if he cannot find some word of God which will more surely and safely carry him.' 'Some word of God': it has come to us; crowning the legitimate efforts, supplying the inevitable deficiencies of human reasoning; satisfying all the deepest aspirations of the heart and conscience. It has come to us, and not as a mere spoken message, but as an incarnate person, at first to attract, to alarm, to subdue us; afterwards, when we are His servants, to guide, to discipline, to enlighten, to enrich us, till that which is perfect is come, and that which is in part shall be done away." Aye, this is it which meets every longing of our hearts. We shall be like Him when we see Him as He is.

Oh, toil-worn pilgrim, weary with your burden, would you know the glory in store for you? Look at Jesus: you shall be like Him. Are you tempted to despair? Do you shrink from an endless future in which you shall remain for ever yourself? Look at Jesus: not as you are, but like what He is, you are to be. If we can but attain to such a hope, heaven bursts at once upon our souls. To be like Jesus! Is this not a glory, in the presence of which all other glories fade away by reason of the glory that is surpassing? When we look at Jesus, we may not—we cannot afford to—forget that we are looking at that which, by the grace of God, we may and shall become.

And you, in whose veins the pulses of youth are still beating, whose hearts are high as you look out upon the still untrodden fields of life—fields which you doubt not you are to subdue—you, all of you, no doubt, have your ideals and your heroes. Some figure rises before your eyes, now as I speak to you, whom you would fain be like—a soldier, a thinker, some master of assemblies, some leader of men, some lord of finance. Or, perhaps, your gentler blood throbs with exhilarated longing as you fancy yourself repeating in your own life the strivings or the accomplishments of some noble woman of history or of romance—some high-minded Hypatia, some patient Griselda, some devoted Saint Catharine—a Florence Nightingale, an Elizabeth Fry, a Dora Pattison, a Frances Havergal. What would it be to you to have an angel visitant stand suddenly by your side—as long ago there stood suddenly by Mary, most blessed of women, one with the greeting on his lips of "Hail Mary! thou that art highly favored!"—and say, "Your wish is granted; this—all this—you shall be!" Are we so blind that we do not see that this, and more, is just what has come to us? All these heroes of our hearts, great and inspiring as they are, are but men and women like ourselves, touched with our faults, our failings, our sins. Partial and incomplete, alike in themselves and in their accomplishments, they can provide us with but stepping-stones to higher things. The one perfect man, the one perfect model of life, stands before us in Christ Jesus. And the voice comes to us—not the voice of an angel only, but God's own voice of power—proclaiming, Ye shall be like Him!

Could there be another proclamation of equal encouragement, of equal strengthening? Up, brethren, let us take Him, the perfect One, for our model; let us nurse our longing to be like Him; and let us go forth to the work of life buoyant with the joy of this greatest of hopes, this most precious of assurances—We shall be like Him; what He is, that shall we also become! In the strength of this great hope let us live our life out here below, and in its joyful assurance let us, when our time comes to go, enter eagerly into our glory.

II

THE SAVING CHRIST

II

THE SAVING CHRIST

"Faithful is the saying, and worthy of all acceptation, that Christ Jesus came into the world to save sinners."—1 TIM. i. 15. (R. V.)

IN these words we have the first of a short series of five "faithful sayings," or current Christian commonplaces, incidentally adduced by the apostle Paul in the course of his letters to his helpers in the gospel—Timothy and Titus—*i. e.*, in what we commonly call his Pastoral Epistles. They are a remarkable series of five "words," and their appearance on the face of these New Testament writings is almost as remarkable as their contents.

Consider what the phenomenon is that is brought before us in these "faithful sayings." Here is the apostle writing to his assistants in the proclamation of the gospel, little more than a third of a century, say, after the crucifixion of his Lord —scarcely thirty-three years after he had himself entered upon the great ministry that had been committed to him of preaching to the Gentiles the words of this life. Yet he is already able to remind them of the blessed contents of the gospel message in words that are the product of Christian experience in the hearts of the community. For just what these "faithful sayings" are, is a body of utterances in which the essence of the gospel has been crystallized by those who have tasted and seen its preciousness. Obviously the days when this gospel was brought as a novelty to their attention are past. The church has been founded, and in it throbs the pulses of a vigorous life. The gospel has been embraced and lived; it has been trusted and not found wanting; and the souls that have found its blessedness have had time to frame its precious truths into formulas. Formulas, I do not say, merely, that have passed from mouth to mouth, and been enshrined in memory after memory until they have become proverbs in the Christian community. Formulas rather, which have embedded themselves in the hearts of the whole congregation, have been beaten there into shape, as the deeper emotions of redeemed souls have played round them, and have emerged again suffused with the feelings which they have awakened and satisfied, and molded into that balanced and rhythmic form which is the hallmark of utterances that come really out of the living and throbbing hearts of the people.

If we were to judge of the spiritual attainments of the primitive Church solely by these specimens of its Christian thought, we should assuredly conceive exceedingly highly of them. Where can we go to find a truer or deeper insight into the heart of the gospel—a richer or fuller expression of all that the religious life at its highest turns upon? Certainly not to the apocryphal fragments of so-called "utterances of Jesus" raked out of the trash-heaps of some Oxyrhynchus or other. But just as truly not to the authentic remains of the early ages of the Church; which witness, indeed, to a living, vitalizing Christianity ordering all its life, but which distinctly reach to no such level of Christian thinking and feeling as these fragments point to. We are thus bidden to remember that in these five "sayings" we have, not the total product of the Christian thought of the age, perhaps not even a fair sample of it, but such items of it only as commended themselves to the mind and heart of a Paul, and rose joyously to his lips when he would fain exhort his fellows in the gospel to embrace and live by its essence. They come to us accordingly not merely as valuable fragments of the Christian thinking of the first period—of absorbing interest as they would be even from that point of view—but with the imprimatur of the apostle upon them as consonant with the mind of the Holy Spirit. They are dug from the mine of the Christian heart indeed, but they come to us stamped in the mintage of apostolic authority. The primitive Christian community it may have been that gave them form and substance, but it is the apostle who assures us that they are "faithful sayings, and worthy of all acceptation."

And surely, when we come to look narrowly at the particular one of these "sayings" which we have chosen as our text, it is a great assertion that it brings us—an assertion which, if it be truly a "faithful saying, and worthy of all acceptation," is well adapted to become even in this late and, it would fain believe itself, more instructed age, the watchword of the Christian Church and of every Christian heart. On the face of it, you will observe, it simply announces the purpose or, we may perhaps say, the philosophy, of the incarnation: "This is a faithful saying, and worthy of all acceptation, that Christ Jesus came into the world to save sinners." But it announces the purpose of the incarnation in a manner that at once attracts attention. Even the very language in which it is expressed is startling, meeting us here in the midst of one of Paul's letters. For this is not Pauline phraseology that stands before us here; as, indeed, it professes not to be—for does not Paul tell us that he is not speaking in his own person, but is adducing one of the jewels of the Church's faith? At all events, it is the language of John that here confronts us, and whoever first cast the Church's heart-conviction into this compressed sentence had assuredly learned in John's school. For to John only belongs this phrase as applied to Christ: "He came into the world." It is John only who preserves the Master's declarations: "I came forth from the Father, and am come into the world"; "I am come a light into the world, that whosoever believeth on Me should not abide in darkness." It is he only who, adopting, as is his wont, the very phraseology of his Master to express his own thought, tells us in his prologue that "the true Light—that lighteth every man—was coming into the world," but though He was in the world, and the world was made by Him, yet the world knew Him not.

Hence emerges a useful hint for the interpretation of our passage. For in the Johannean phraseology which we have before us here—though certainly not in the Johannean phraseology only—the term "the world" does not express a purely local idea, but is suffused with a deep ethical significance. When we read accordingly of Christ Jesus coming into the "world," we are not reading of a mere change of place on the part of our Lord—of a mere descent on His part from heaven to earth, as we may say. We are reading of the light coming into the darkness: "the world" is the sphere of darkness and shame and sin. It is, in a word, the great ethical contrast that is intended to be brought prominently before us, and in this lies the whole point of the incarnation as conceived by John, and as embodied in our passage. Jesus Christ, the Lord of glory, came into "the world"—into the realm of evil and the kingdom of sin. In our present passage this idea is enhanced by the sharp collocation with it of the term "sinners." For, in the original, the word "sinners" stands next to the word "world," with the effect of throwing the strongest possible emphasis on the ethical connotation. This is the faithful saying, and worthy of all acceptation, that the apostle commends to us —that "Christ Jesus came into the *world, sinners* to save." What else, indeed, could He have come into "the world," the sphere of evil, for—except to save sinners?

Surely, there meets us here a point that is worthy of our closest attention. We might have heard of Christ coming into the world, if the term could be taken in a merely local sense, with but a languid interest. But when we catch the ethical import of the term an explanation is at once demanded. What could such an one as Christ have to do in coming to such a place as the world? The incongruity of the thing requires accounting for. It is much as if we saw a fellow Christian in some compromising position. We might meet with him here, there, and elsewhere, and no remark be aroused. But by some chance swing of the shutter as we pass by we see him standing in the midst of a drinking-saloon; we see him emerge from the door of a well-known gambling hell, or of some dreadful abode of shame. At once the need of an explanation rises within our puzzled minds, and the whole stress of the situation turns on the explanation. What was his purpose there? we anxiously inquire. So it is with Christ Jesus coming into the world; and so we feel in proportion as we realize the ethical contrariety suggested by the term. Thus it comes about that the primary emphasis of the passage is felt to rest on the account it gives of the situation it brings before us—on its explanation of how it happens that Christ Jesus could and did come into the world.

We despair of finding an English phraseology which will reproduce with exactitude the nice distribution of the stress. Suffice it to say that the strong emphasis falls on the fact that it was specifically *to save sinners* that Christ Jesus came, and that the way for this strength of emphasis is prepared by the use of phraseology which implies that there was no other conceivable end that He could have had in view in coming into such a place as the world except to deal with sinners, of which the world consists. He might indeed have come to judge the world; and in contrast with that the emphasis falls on the word "to *save*." But He could not conceivably, being what He was, the Holy One and the Just, have come to such a place as the world is—the seat of shame and evil—save to deal with *sinners*. The essence of the whole declaration, therefore, is found in the joyful cry that it was specifically *to save sinners* that Christ Jesus came into this world of evil. And if that be true—simply true, broadly true, true just as it stands, and in all the reach of its meaning—why, then, from that alone we may learn what man is and what God is—what Christ Jesus is and His work in this world of ours—what hopes may illumine our darkness here below, and what joys shall be ours when this darkness passes away.

It would naturally be impossible for us to dip out all the fullness of such a great declaration in a half-hour's meditation. It will be profitable for us, accordingly, to confine ourselves to bringing as clearly before us as may prove to be practicable two or three of its main implications. And may God the Holy Spirit help us to read it aright and to apply its lessons to our souls' welfare!

First of all, then, let us observe that this "faithful saying" takes us back into the counsels of eternity and reveals to us the ground, in the decree of God, for the gift of His Son to the world, and the end sought to be obtained by His entrance into the likeness of sinful flesh. "Faithful is the saying," says the apostle, "and worthy of all acceptation, that Christ Jesus came into the world *in order to save sinners.*" That is to say, the occasion of the incarnation is rooted in sin, and the end of it is found in salvation from sin. And that is to say again, translating these facts into the terms of the decree, that the determination of God to send His Son and the determination of the Son to come into the world are grounded, in the counsel of God, on the contemplated fact of sin, and have as their design to provide a remedy for sin.

This, it need hardly be said, is in accordance with the uniform representation of Scripture. Scripture always speaks of the incarnation as the hinge of a great remedial scheme. Our Lord Himself, in language closely parallel to that be-before us, says, "The Son of man is come to seek and to save that which was lost." And everywhere in Scripture the incarnation is conceived distinctly, if we may be permitted the use of these technical terms, soteriologically rather than ontologically, or even cosmologically. Under the guidance of Scripture, and preëminently of our present passage, therefore, we must needs deny that the proximate account of the incarnation is to be sought either ontologically or ethically in God, or in the nature of the Logos, or in the idea of creation, or in the character of man as created; and affirm that it is to be found only in the needy condition of man as a sinner before the face of a holy and loving God.

The incarnation, to be sure, is so stupendous an event that it is big with consequences, and reaches out on every side to relations that may seem at first glance even to stand in opposition to its fundamental principle. It is certainly true that all that is, is the product of God's power, and, as coming from Him, has somewhat of God in it and may be envisaged by us as a vehicle of the Divine. And surely it is only true that He has imprinted Himself on the works of His hands; and that, as the Author of all, He will not be content with the product of His power until it has been made to body forth all His perfections; and it cannot be wrong to say that so far as we can see it is only in an incarnation that He could manifest Himself perfectly to His creatures. A similar remark will apply naturally at once also to the Logos as the Revealer, who must be supposed to desire to make known to man all that God is, and preëminently His love, which undoubtedly lies at the basis of the incarnation, and may be properly represented as its very principle and impulsive cause. Nor can it be doubted that only in his union with God in Christ, which is the result of Christ's incarnated work, does man reach his true destiny—the destiny designed for him from the beginning of the world, and without which in prospect, so far as we can see, man would never have been created at all.

But it is of the utmost importance for us to

observe that these truths, great and fundamental as they are, yet do not penetrate to the basal fact as to the end of the incarnation. Nor can they safely be treated atomistically as so many independent truths unrelated to one another or to the real principle of the incarnation. They rather form parts of one complete sphere of truth whose center lies in the soteriological incarnation of the Bible. And only as each finds its proper place as a segment of this sphere of truth formed about that great fact does it possess validity, or even attain the height of its own idea. It is only, for example, because Christ Jesus came to save sinners that all that God is is manifested in Him, that love finds its completest exhibition in Him, that through Him at last man attains his primal destiny. Eliminate sin as the proximate occasion and redemption as the prime end of the incarnation, and none of these other effects will follow from it at all, or at least not in the measure of their rights. So that it is only true to say that in order that each may attain its proper place in our contemplation, as we seek to gather together the ends served by the incarnation, it is essential that they be conceived not apart from salvation from sin, the primary end of the incarnation, as its substitutes, but along with it, as its complements.

But this great declaration not only takes us back into the counsels of the eternal God that we may learn what from the ages of ages He purposed for sinful man, but it also throws an intense emphasis on the nature of the work which the incarnate Son of God came to perform. We require only to adjust the stress that falls on the separate words a little more precisely to catch a new meaning in its inspiring words, which declare that Christ Jesus came into the world to *save sinners*.

What, after all, are we looking for in Christ? Perhaps very divergent replies might be returned to this query did we but probe our hearts deeply enough and question our hopes resolutely enough. At all events, from the very earliest ages of Christianity, men have approached Him with very varied needs prominent in their minds, and have sought in Him satisfaction for very diverse necessities. They have felt the need of a teacher, an example, a revealer of God, a manifestation of the Divine love, an unveiling of the mysteries of the spiritual world, or of the life that lies beyond the grave. Or they have felt the need of a protector, a strong governor on whose arm they could rest, a bulwark against the evils of this life, and a tower of strength for their support and safety, whether in this life or in that to come. Or they have felt the need of a ransom from sin, of a redeemer, an expiation, a reconciler with God, a sanctifier. In the opulent provision for all that man can require made in the work of the Son of man, we can find all this, and more, in Him. But it makes every difference where, amid the rich profusion of His mercies, we discover the center of gravity of the benefits conferred on us, and what we ascribe more to the periphery.

In particular, in the first age of the gospel declaration it appealed to men more especially along three lines of deeply felt needs. Some, oppressed chiefly by their sense of the ignorance of God and of spiritual realities in which they had languished in the days of their heathendom, and dazzled by the light of the glorious gospel He brought to them, looked to Christ most eagerly as the Logos, the great Revealer, who had brought the knowledge of God to them, and with the knowledge of God the knowledge of themselves also as the sons of God. Others, oppressed rather by the miseries of life, turned from the dreadful physical and social conditions in which humanity itself had nearly been ground out of them, to hail in Christ the founder of a new social order; and permitted their quickened hopes to play almost exclusively round the promises of the kingdom He had come to establish and the joys it would bring. We call the one class "Gnostics" and the other "Chiliasts"; and by the very attribution to them of these party names indicate our clear perception that in neither of these channels did the great stream of Christian faith run. For from the beginning it has been true of Christians at large that the evils they have looked to Christ primarily to be relieved from have been neither intellectual nor social, but rather distinctly moral and spiritual. There have arisen from time to time one-sided and insufficient modes of expressing even this deeper longing and truer trust in Christ. Early Christians were apt, for example, to speak of themselves too exclusively as under bondage to Satan, and to look to Christ as a ransom to Satan for their release. But, however strangely they may now and again have expressed themselves, the essence of the matter lay clearly revealed in their thought —this, namely, in the words of the text, that Christ Jesus had come into the world to *save sinners*; that sin is the evil from which we need deliverance, and that it was to redeem from sin that the Son of God left His throne and companied with wicked men for a season.

The two thousand years of Christian life that have been lived since the gospel of salvation was brought into the world have not availed to eliminate from His Church these insufficient conceptions of our Lord's work. Even in this twentieth century of ours there still exist Christian intellectualists as extreme as any Gnostic of old: men who look to Christ for nothing but instruction, manifestation, revelation, teaching, example; and who still discover the essence of Christianity in the higher and better knowledge it brings of what is true and good and beautiful. And by their side there still exist to-day Christian socialists as extreme as any Chiliast of old: men whose whole talk is of the amelioration of life brought about by Christ, of the salvation of society, of the establishment on Christian principles of a new social order and the upbuilding of a new social structure; and whose prime hope in Christ is for the relief of the distresses of life and the building up of a kingdom of well-being in the world.

We shall be in no danger, of course, of neglecting the truth that is embodied in the intellectualistic and the socialistic gospels. Christ is our Prophet and our King. He did come to make us know what God is, and what His purposes of mercy are to men; and where the light of that knowledge is shut out from men's sight how great is the darkness and how great is the misery of that darkness! He is our wisdom, our teacher beyond compare. So far from minimizing either the extent or the value of His revelations, we must rather acknowledge that we cannot magnify them enough. And Christ did come to implant in human society a new principle of social health and organization, and the leaven which He has thus imbedded in the mass is working, and is destined to continue to work, every conceivable improvement in the structure of society until the whole is leavened. In a word, Christ did come to found a kingdom, and in that kingdom men shall dwell together in amity and peace, and love shall be its law, and happiness its universal condition. It is with no desire to minimize the intellectual and social blessings that Christ has brought the world, therefore, that we would insist that the center of His work lies elsewhere. We all the more heartily hail Him as our Prophet and our King, that we must insist that He is also, and above all, our Priest. He has saved us from ignorance; He has saved us from pain; but these are not the evils on which the hinge of His saving work turns. Above all and before all He has saved us from sin. "Faithful is the saying, and worthy of all acceptation, that Christ Jesus came into the world to save *sinners.*"

And it is only by saving us from sin, we must further remark, that He saves us from ignorance and from misery. There is a high and true sense, valid here too, in the saying that faith precedes reason: that it is only he that is in Christ Jesus who can know God and acquire any effective insight into spiritual truth. And equally in that other maxim that the regeneration of the individual is the condition of the regeneration of society: that it is only he that is in Christ Jesus who can have added to him even these lesser benefits. Apart from the central salvation from sin, knowledge can but puff up, and society at best is a whited sepulchre, full of dead men's bones. And it is only by His prime work of saving from sin—that sin which is the root of all our ignorance and of all our bitterness alike—that He makes the tree good that its fruits may be good also. In the penetrating declaration of our text, therefore, we perceive the heart of Christianity uncovered for us. The saying that it was to save sinners that Christ Jesus came into

THE SAVING CHRIST

the world is a faithful one, and worthy of all acceptation. And that means that it is not the primary function of Christianity in the world to educate men, though we shall not get along without teaching; or to ameliorate their physical and social condition, though we shall not get along without charity; but to proclaim salvation from sin. It exists in the world not for making men wise, nor for making them comfortable, but for saving them from sin. That done and all is done—each result following in its due course. That not done, and nothing is done. All the wisdom of the ages, all the delights of life, are of no avail so long as we are oppressed with sin. The core of the gospel is assuredly that Christ Jesus came to save *sinners*.

We need, however, once more to adjust the emphasis more precisely in order to gain the whole message of our passage. What Paul declares to be a faithful saying, and worthy of all acceptation, is that Christ Jesus came to *save* sinners. Put the emphasis now on the one word "*save*"—Christ Jesus came to *save* sinners.

Not, then, merely to prepare salvation for them; to open to them a pathway to salvation; to remove the obstacles in the way of their salvation;

to proclaim as a teacher a way of salvation; to introduce as a ruler conditions of life in which clean living becomes for the first time possible; to bring motives to holy action to bear upon us; to break down our enmity to God by an exhibition of His seeking love; to manifest to us what sin is in the sight of God, and how He will visit it with His displeasure. All these things He undoubtedly does. But all these things together touch but the circumference of His work for man. Under no interpretation of the nature or reach of His work can it be truly said that Christ Jesus *came* to do these things. For that we must penetrate deeper, and say with the primitive Church, in this faithful saying commended to us by the apostle, that Christ Jesus came to *save* sinners.

We must take the great declaration in the height and depth of its tremendous meaning. Jesus did all that is included in the great word "*save.*" He did not come to induce us to save ourselves, or to help us to save ourselves, or to enable us to save ourselves. He came to *save* us. And it is therefore that His name was called Jesus—because He should save His people from their sins. The glory of our Lord, surpassing all His other glories to usward, is just that He is our actual and complete Saviour; our Saviour to the uttermost. Our knowledge, even though it be His gift to us as our Prophet, is not our saviour, be it as wide and as deep and as high as it is possible to conceive. The Church, though it be His gift to us as our King, is not our saviour, be it as holy and true as it becomes the Church, the bride of the Lamb, to be. The reorganized society in which He has placed us, though it be the product of His holy rule over the redeemed earth, is not our saviour, be it the new Jerusalem itself, clothed in its beauty and descended from heaven. Nay, let us cut more deeply still. Our faith itself, though it be the bond of our union with Christ through which we receive all His blessings, is not our saviour. We have but one Saviour; and that one Saviour is Jesus Christ our Lord. Nothing that we are and nothing that we can do enters in the slightest measure into the ground of our acceptance with God. Jesus did it all. And by doing it all He has become in the fullest and widest and deepest sense the word can bear—our *Saviour*. For this end did He come into the world—to *save* sinners; and nothing short of the actual and complete *saving* of sinners will satisfy the account of His work given by His own lips and repeated from them by all His apostles.

It is in this great fact, indeed, that there lies the

whole essence of the gospel. For let us never forget that the gospel is not *good advice*, but *good news*. It does not come to us to make known to us what we must do to earn salvation for ourselves, but proclaiming to us what Jesus has done to save us. It is salvation, a completed salvation, that it announces to us; and the burden of its message is just the words of our text—that Christ Jesus came into the world to *save* sinners.

Now Paul could never write of this tremendously moving truth in a cold and dry spirit. There was nothing that so burned in his soul as his profound sense of his indebtedness to his Redeemer for his entire salvation. We cannot be surprised, therefore, to note that as he repeats these great words, "Christ Jesus came into the world to *save* sinners," his thought reverts at once to his own part in this great salvation; and he cries aloud with swelling heart, "Of whom I am chief." Says an old Anglican writer: "The apostle applies the worst word in the text to himself." But we must punctually note, Paul is not, therefore, boasting of his sin. He is, on the contrary, glorying in his salvation. If Christ came just to save sinners, he says, in effect, Why that means me; for that is what I am. There is a sense, then, no doubt, in which he can be said to be glad that he can claim to be a sinner. Not because he delights in wickedness, but because that places him within the reach of the mission of Him who Himself declared that He came not to call the righteous, but sinners. Paul knows there is deep-seated evil within him; he knows his own inability to remedy it—for does not that long life of legalistic struggle, when after the straitest sect of his religion he lived a Pharisee, witness to his agonizing efforts to heal his deadly hurt? In Christ Jesus, who came to save sinners, he sees the one hope of sinners like himself; and with deep revulsion of feeling he takes his willing place among sinners that he may take his place also among saved sinners. His only comfort in life and death is found in the fact that Christ Jesus came just to save sinners.

Brethren, it is there only also that our comfort can be found, whether for life or for death. Perhaps even yet we hardly know, as we should know, our need of a saviour. Perhaps we may acknowledge ourselves to be sinners only in languid acquiescence in a current formula. Such a state of self-ignorance cannot, however, last for ever. And some day—probably it has already come to most of us—some day the scales will fall from our eyes, and we shall see ourselves as we really are. Ah, then, we shall have no difficulty in placing ourselves by the apostle's side, and pronouncing ourselves, in the accents of the deepest conviction, the chief of sinners. And, then, *our* only comfort for life and death, too, will be in the discovery that Christ Jesus came into the world just to save sinners. We may have long admired Him as a teacher sent from God, and have long sought to serve Him as a King re-ordering the world; but we shall find in that great day of self-discovery that we have never known Him at all till He has risen upon our soul's vision as our Priest, making His own body a sacrifice for our sin. For such as we shall then know ourselves to be, it is only as a Saviour from sin that Christ will suffice; and we will passionately make our own such words as these that a Christian singer has put into our mouths:—

> "I sought thee, weeping, high and low,
> I found Thee not; I did not know
> I was a sinner—even so,
>   I missed Thee for my Saviour.
>
> "I saw Thee sweetly condescend
> Of humble men to be the friend,
> I chose Thee for my way, my end,
>   But found Thee not my Saviour,

"Until upon the cross I saw
My God, who died to meet the law
That man had broken; then I saw
My sin, and then my Saviour.

"What seek I longer? let me be
A sinner all my days to Thee,
Yet more and more, and Thee to me
Yet more and more my Saviour.

* * * * * * *

"Be Thou to me my Lord, my Guide,
My Friend, yea, everything beside;
But first, last, best, whate'er betide
Be Thou to me my Saviour!"

III

THE ARGUMENT FROM EXPERIENCE

III

THE ARGUMENT FROM EXPERIENCE

"Therefore being justified by faith, we have peace with God through our Lord Jesus Christ, . . . and rejoice in hope of the glory of God."—ROM. v. 1, 2 (A. V.).

THE subject of these two verses is the Christian's peace and joy. You will observe that the apostle does not argue that a Christian ought to have peace and joy. He does not exhort Christians to seek to attain peace and joy. He does not expound the nature of a Christian's peace and joy. He does something far more striking. He assumes the Christian's peace and joy as a fact of experience, the unquestionable reality of which may stand as a common ground of reasoning between him and his readers. He thus represents peace and joy as a special characteristic of Christians, recognized as such by all—peace of heart as a present possession, and joy over the great hope which is theirs for the future. "We have," says he, "peace with God, and we rejoice over the hope of the glory of God."

Upon this fact, adduced here just because it

is a universally acknowledged and undeniable fact, that the Christian enjoys this peace with God and with happy lips exults over the hope of glory, the apostle founds an argument. Let us recall the place of the passage in the general disposition of the matter in the epistle. In the opening chapters was exhibited the necessity of a justification by faith and not by works. Then the nature and working of this method of salvation was expounded. Then the apostle begins a series of arguments designed to show that this is indeed God's method of saving men. The first proof that he offers is drawn from the case of Abraham, and operates to show that God has always so dealt with His people: for that Abraham, the father of the faithful, was justified by faith and not by works the Scriptures expressly testify, saying that "Abraham *believed* God, and it was accounted to him unto righteousness." This is the immediately preceding section to our present passage. In the immediately succeeding section he appeals to the analogy of God's dealings with men in other matters. It was by the trespass of one that men were brought into sin and death —does it not comport with God's methods that by the righteousness of one men should be brought into justification and life? Our present passage lies between, and constitutes an intermediate argument that justification by faith is God's own method of saving sinners.

This argument, you will observe, is drawn from the experience of Paul's Christian readers. They had made trial of this method of salvation; they had sought justification, not on the ground of works of righteousness which they could do, but out of faith. And the turmoil of guilty dread before God which filled their hearts had sunk into a sweet sense of peace, and the future to which they had hitherto looked shudderingly forward in fearful expectation of judgment had taken on a new aspect—they "exult in hope of the glory of God." It is on this, their own experience, that the apostle fixes their eyes. They have sought justification out of faith; they have reaped the fruits of justification in peace and joy. Can they doubt the reality of the middle term, of that justification that mediates between their faith and their peace and joy? As well tell the famishing wanderer that the pool into which he has dipped his cup is but a mirage of the desert, when from it the refreshing fluid is already pouring over his parched tongue, and bringing life and vigor into every languid member. "It is because we have been justified," says the apostle—and here is the emphasis, "the triumphant emphasis," as the great German commentator H. A. W. Meyer puts it—" it is because we have been really and actually justified out of faith, that we have this peace with God, and are able to exult in the hope of the glory of God." Thus the apostle argues back from their conscious peace and joy to the reality of the justification out of which they grow.

It is very interesting to observe this prominent use in the reasoning of the apostle Paul of what we have learned to call "the argument from experience." Some appear to fancy this argument one of the greatest discoveries of the nineteenth century; others look upon it with suspicion as if its use were an innovation of dangerous tendency. No doubt, like other forms of argumentation, it is liable to misuse. It is to misuse it to confound it with proof by experiment. By his use of the argument from experience Paul is far from justifying those who will accept as true only those elements of the Christian faith the truth of which they can verify by experiment. There is certainly an easily recognizable difference between trusting God for the future because we have known His goodness in the past, and casting ourselves from every pinnacle of the temple of truth in turn to see whether He has really given His angels charge concerning us, according to His word.

And what misuse of this argument could be more fatal than to make it carry the whole weight of the evidences of our religion, or even, as has sometimes been done, to attempt to enhance its value by disparaging all other methods of proof? Such an exaggeration of its importance is a symptom of that unhappy subjectivity in religion unfortunately growing in our modern Church, which betrays its weakened hold upon the objective truth and reality of Christianity by its neglect or even renunciation of the objective proofs of its truth. No wonder when men find the philosophical principles or critical postulates to which they have committed their thinking, working their way subtilely but surely into every detail of their thought, and gradually taking from them their confidence in those supernatural facts on which Christianity rests—no wonder, I say, that in such circumstances they should despairingly declare that the essence of Christianity is independent of its supposed supernatural history, and is vindicated by the imminent experiences of their own souls. Needless to say that the essence of Christianity which in their view is proved by their experiences is not the Christianity of Christ and His apostles, but the philosophical faith of their own preconceptions. And needless to say that this despairing and exclusive use of the argument from experience has no analogy in the usage of Paul. With him, it takes its place among the other arguments, and is not permitted to take the place of the rest. He appeals first to God's announced intention from the beginning so to deal with His people, and to the historic fact of His so dealing with them. And he appeals last to the analogy of His dealings with men in other matters. Between these he places the argument from experience, and twines the strong cord of his proof from the three fibers of God's express promise, our experience, and the analogy of His working. When we unite the Scriptural, experiential, and analogical arguments we are followers of Paul.

Such a use of the argument from experience by Paul, though it may interest us, certainly cannot surprise us. It is no unwonted thing with Paul. It constantly appears in his writings as a capital argument, and such was his confidence in it that he did not hesitate at times to stake much upon its validity. It is to this argument, for example, that he appeals when he cries to the foolish Galatians: "This only would I know from you, Received ye the Spirit by works of law or by the hearing of faith?" They had received the Spirit —of that he and they alike were sure. And they had sought Him, not by law-works, but by faith. That, too, they knew very well. Were they so foolish as to be unable to draw the inference thrust upon them—that the seeking that found was the true and right seeking? The apostle will then draw it for them. "He therefore that supplieth the Spirit to you, and worketh powers in you, doeth He it by law-works or by the hearing of faith? Even as Abraham believed God, and it was reckoned to him unto righteousness. Ye perceive, therefore, that they which be of faith, the same are Abraham's sons."

An humbler servant of Christ than Paul, and a far earlier one, had, indeed, long before pressed this argument with matchless force. Blind unbelief alone could say to him who once was blind but now could see: "This man is not from God. Give glory to God; we know that this man is a sinner." The one, the sufficient answer was: "Whether He be a sinner, I know not; one thing I know, that whereas I was blind, now I see. . . . Why herein is the marvel, that ye know not whence He is, and yet He opened mine eyes!" Greater marvel than the opening of the eyes of one born blind that men should shut their eyes to who, and what, and whence He is, who opens blind eyes! "If this man were not from God, He could do nothing!"

What, after all, is this "argument from experience" but an extension of our Lord's favorite argument from the fruits to the tree which bears the fruits? He who is producing the fruits of the Spirit has received the Spirit; he who has reaped the fruits of justification has received justification; and he who has obtained these fruits by the seeking of faith knows that he has obtained out of his faith the justification of which they are the fruits; and may know, therefore, that the way of faith is the right and true way of obtaining justification. We must not pause in the midst of the argument and refuse to draw the final conclusion. If the presence of the fruits of justification proves we are justified, the presence of the justification, thus proved, proves that justification is found on the road by which we reached it. This is the apostle's argument.

That the argument is valid it is not easy to doubt. It is one of those practical appeals which carry conviction even to minds which do not care to investigate the grounds of their validity. Nevertheless its validity has its implications, and this is as much as to say that it rests on presuppositions without which it would not be valid. Men may draw water from a well and be assured that it comes to them through the action of the pump, without at all understanding, or stopping to consider, the theory of suction by which the pump acts. But no pump will yield water if it be not constructed in accordance with the principles of suction. And it seems accordingly important that the principles of suction should be understood. Our understanding of these principles not only increases the intelligence but also adds to the confidence with which we accredit the refreshing floods to its gift. In a somewhat analogous way it will repay us to investigate the validity of the apostle's argument from experience, and to seek to bring clearly before us the presuppositions on which its validity rests and the lines of reasoning on which its conclusions may be justified. It will surely grow in force to us in proportion to the clearness with which its implications are apprehended.

These implications or presuppositions are, speaking broadly, two. In the first place, it is implied in the validity of this argument—so immediately and inevitably recognized—that there is a natural adaptation in this mode of salvation —the mode of justification by faith—for the production of peace and joy in the heart of the sinner that embraces it. And in the second place, it is implied in the validity of this argument that the deliverances of the human conscience are but the shadows of the divine judgment: that its imperatives repeat the demands of God's righteousness, and its satisfaction argues the satisfaction of the divine justice. Let us look at these implications in turn.

First, let us inquire if there is not necessarily implied a natural adaptation in justification by faith to produce peace and joy in the sinner.

We have sought, let us say, justification out of faith. We have peace and joy. Here are two facts. We may look at them separately. What is to unite them in our apprehension? What warrants us to infer from the mere fact that we have peace and joy that this peace and joy are the product of the justification that we have sought out of faith, and therefore argue the reality of that justification and the success of our seeking it by faith?

Is it merely that the peace and joy have succeeded in the sequence of time the seeking by faith? What is to assure us that this is not a mere *post hoc* and no *propter hoc* at all? Is it then merely the universality of the experience—our observation that all such seekers have proved to be finders? Is a Christian to base his peace and joy, then, on another's finding? Nay, on the invariableness of such finding by others? Who will assure him of this invariableness? Who will assure him that the next seeker may not fail to find? That in the next village such seekers may not as invariably fail as among his own acquaintances they have invariably found? That his partial observation, in a word, is the norm of fact? Must he wait to base his confidence and hope on the collection and tabulation of a body of statistics?

For the validity of the argument it is obvious that there must be some more immediate and obvious vinculum between the seeking and finding than mere observed sequence, some natural connection between the justification sought by faith and the peace and joy which have come to the seeker—level to the apprehension of all, and pointing each one directly to his justification, as the source of his peace and joy, in so clear and convincing a way that he needs must find the account of his inward peace in the reality of his outward justification. Does any such connection exist?

Something of this connection will no doubt be supplied by the fact that these Christians who now enjoy this peace and joy have been seekers of peace and joy by other methods than through faith, and have not found; and only upon laying aside their feverish efforts at self-salvation and upon seeking through faith, have they found. The contrast of these diverse experiences counts for much, and assures them that the blessed fruits of justification ripen in the heart only when justification is sought through faith; that they do not grow on the tree of works. Were this not the experience of Christians, the apostle's whole argument would fail. That argument has, therefore, a double edge; it as much implies that peace and joy do not come through works as that they do come through faith. What he is attempting to prove is just that justification comes out of faith and not out of works; and the experience it rests upon must be an experience, therefore, of not finding as truly as an experience of finding. This double experience, then, we say, will go far toward connecting the peace and joy

THE ARGUMENT FROM EXPERIENCE 69

which Christians possess, with a justification specifically by faith as its root and source.

It will go far toward it, but it will not go the whole way. The connection so found is still only an empirical one. Even if it should prove universal it might still be accidental. A deeper fact must lie behind, creating a more necessary connection; or rather, let us say, giving a rational account of this experience. That deeper fact must lie in some inherent difference in the modes of seeking; that is, it can only lie in the natural adaptation of the mode of salvation set forth in the term "justification by faith" for the production of peace and joy in the heart of the sinner who embraces it—a natural adaptation absent from works. In other words, the connection will fully emerge only on the discovery of the fact that peace and joy are the natural, or, indeed, the necessary fruits of seeking salvation in the method proclaimed by the apostle.

In order to make this plain, we have only to formulate clearly the question on the decision of which it is suspended. It is this: Whether there is an adaptation in the method of salvation proclaimed by Paul for the production of such effects as peace and joy: or whether the peace and joy which follow the trial of this mode of salvation arise within the heart wholly unrelated with, and pointing in no wise back to, the justification of which they are the fruits. In other words, whether men find peace and joy on seeking justification through faith only because the Holy Spirit works these sentiments in some mysterious way in their hearts—causing them to spring up within them on His almighty fiat as flowers growing on no stalk; or whether the Spirit's fecundating power causes them to grow visibly upon the stem of justification by faith itself. We cannot doubt, following Paul, which is the true alternative.

The sense of peace that steals into the heart, the exulting joy which cannot keep silence on the lips of him who seeks his justification out of faith, are indeed the work of the Holy Spirit. Apart from His vitalizing operations even the saved soul might remain dark and the redeemed lips dumb. But they do not, therefore, hang in the air without cognizable ground or source. The Holy Spirit does not here, any more than in other spheres of his activity, work irrational effects. There is a rational account to be given of this peace and joy as well as a spiritual one. The mode of justification propounded by God through the apostle is one which is adapted to the actual condition of man; one which is calculated to satisfy his conscience, to allay his remorseful sense of guilt, to supply him a rational ground of conviction of acceptance with God, and to quicken in him a happy, hopeful outlook upon the future. And it is because this mode of justification is thus calculated to provide a solid ground for peace and joy to the rational understanding that those who seek justification thus and not otherwise acquire, under the quickening influences of the Spirit, a sense of peace with God and a joyful outlook of hope for the future.

No more here than elsewhere does the Spirit of all order work a blind, an ungrounded, an irrational set of emotions in the heart. Did He so, they would scarcely be probative of anything. A set of emotions arising in the soul, no one knows whence, no one knows on what grounds, especially if they were persistent, and in proportion as they were violent, would only vex the soul and cast it into inquietude. It is only because these Spirit-worked emotions of peace and joy attach themselves rationally to the mode of justification by faith that they can point to it as their source, and prove that they who have sought their justification by faith have surely found. The probative power of the actual peace and joy received by the means of this justification is thus dependent upon the rational adaptability of this method of salvation to produce, in those who make trial of it, peace of heart and joy in the prospect of the future. The gist of the whole matter, then, is that this mode of justification may be recognized as supplying the only true and actual justification, because it alone, among all the methods by which men have sought to obtain peace with God, is calculated to satisfy their consciences and to furnish to them a rational ground of hope of acceptance.

How many other ways there are in which men have sought and continue to seek peace! And how little they avail! Let them seek by works—at the best, they can but cry at the last that they are unprofitable servants. The perfect obedience which their hearts tell them, in a voice which will not be gainsaid, is due from them, they know also that they have not rendered, that they cannot render. And the dreadful load of guilt with which their past offenses have burdened their souls, and which their present sins are continually increasing, weighs down their spirits in hopeless despair. While walking this treadmill road of works no peace can possibly visit their hearts; no exultation in the prospective goal can attend their steps. Present anguish, despairing desperation—these are their only possible heritage.

Let them, then, despairingly recognize the hopelessness of a work-righteousness for such creatures as men, and abase themselves in rueful sorrow before God, confessing the blackness of their sin and the utterness of their helplessness, and pleading God's mercy as their only hope. Can remorse, as it bites back upon the soul in memory of its deeds of shame, atone for guilt incurred—condone for continued incompleteness of obedience? Is it not rather the heart rising up against itself in self-disgust, accusing itself before the holy and just God, and dragging away its refuges of lies that it may see the sword of vengeance hanging over it? How can the awakened sense of sin instill peace into the soul? Or the soul's own fierce condemnation of itself open out before it vistas of exulting hope? When our hearts condemn us it is our despair to know that God is greater than our hearts—greater in His flaming hatred of sin, in the strictness of His inquisition, in the certain vengeance of His justice.

Well, then, may God be bribed? Let us heap up our votive offerings upon His altar. Let us continually sing His praises before men—something after the fashion of those Ephesians who stood in the theater and "all with one voice, about the space of two hours, cried out, 'Great is Diana of the Ephesians!'" Let us devote our lives to His service in a perfection of obedience which we know we cannot render, or in an exquisite minuteness of self-torture which we hope He may accept in lieu of obedience. Can we believe that God will accept these in place of His due? Let us drown His altars in the blood of bulls and goats; or—for such is the wont of men seeking to still the accusing voice within them—let us slash our flesh and mingle our own blood with that of the sacrifices. Let us even—for this, too, men have done in their agony of remorse in every corner of this globe—give the fruit of our bodies for the sins of our souls, "making our son or our daughter pass through the fire to Moloch." Or, since those days are passed, and the fires on the world's altars are quenched, let us offer up our own lives to God, starving within us all natural affections, stifling all proper emotions, and painfully immolating ourselves on a daily altar of ascetic observance. Can we believe that thus the righteous anger of the holy and righteous One against our sins will be appeased so that He will satisfy Himself with our imperfect obedience? We know that the judgment of God is true; and that He is of purer eyes than to behold iniquity, even though we writhe in fear before His face and strive to cloud his eyes to its enormity.

But why need we multiply words? Such expedients men have always tried, and such expedients men are everywhere trying, in their despairing search for peace. Every such expedient conceivable men have tried—we have tried—and peace has not been attained. We look in dread about us, and clearly see that every avenue of escape is closed.

Every avenue of escape is closed. All but one. *If*—*if* an adequate atonement might be made for sin; *if* a perfect obedience could be rendered to the law; and *if* this atonement and this obedience should be made ours: then, but only then, could hope awake in our dead souls, could peace once more steal into our troubled hearts. Now, it is just this that Paul offers to a despairing world in the proclamation of justification by faith. It is a proclamation of "justification," you will observe, not a proclamation of escape from sin's penalty—not even a proclamation of simple pardon of sin, or of the eradication of sin—but specifically a proclamation of "justification." It appeals as such to the judgment of conscience, and works its effect in the realm of conscience. Paul does not deny man's guilt—he asserts man's guilt. He does not outrage conscience by proclaiming pardon without expiation of guilt—he proclaims the indefeasible need of expiation. He does not insult intelligence by representing that sinful man can offer the expiation that is required and at the same time acquire merit for reward—he proclaims the helplessness of humanity in its estate of condemnation. He empties us of all righteousness which we may claim, or which we may seek to acquire by our deeds, and proclaims with piercing clearness that by the deeds of the law shall no flesh be justified. And then he turns and points to a wonderful spectacle of the Son of God, become man, taking His place at the head of His people, presenting an infinite sacrifice for their sins in His own body on the tree, working out a perfect righteousness in their stead in the myriad deeds of love and right that filled His short but active life; and offering this righteousness, this righteousness of God, provided by God and acceptable to God, to the acceptance of the world.

Here is a mode of salvation which is indeed calculated to still the gnawing sense of guilt and quiet the fear of wrath. And a capital proof of its truth is that it does at last supply a basis, on which resting, men can believe that they are accepted with God; that it lays a foundation, on which building, men can at length feel peace of heart and entertain hope for the future. In effect the apostle says to his readers: "You have tried every way of making your peace with God: only in this way have you found one which satisfied your consciences. The righteousness of Christ, laid hold of by faith, evidently suffices for all your needs. Resting upon it, your guilty fears subside and you feel safe at last. Thus, and thus alone, you see that God may be just (as you know Him to be unfailingly) and yet the justifier of such sinners as you know yourselves to be."

And you will observe how Paul not only says this in effect in this appeal to his readers' experience, but the whole trend of the epistle up to this point is calculated to give force to the appeal and to evoke an immediate and deep response. For what is that proof, with which the epistle opens, that all men are sinners and under the condemnation of the law, so that the wrath of God is revealed from heaven against them as workers of iniquity, but a faithful probing of conscience, awakening it to a sense of guilt and a consciousness of helplessness? And what is that exposition of God's mode of justification by means of a righteousness provided by Christ and laid hold of by faith, but a loving presentation of the sacrifice and work of Christ to the apprehension of faith? And what is that exposition of the acceptance of Abraham, the father of the faithful, but a gracious assurance that it is thus that God deals mercifully with his children? And what, now, is this appeal to their own experience as they have humbly sought God's forgiveness and acceptance in Christ, by simple faith in Him, but an assault on their hearts, that they may be forced to realize for themselves and confess to their fellow-men all the satisfaction they have found in believing in Christ?

Paul's words, says Jerome, are not like the words of other men, "they have hands and feet"; they are living things and tug at our very heart strings. But they are not less, but more, logical arguments for that; and we perceive that in his present argument it is to this feeling of satisfaction in the man who has sought his justification by believing in Christ that the apostle appeals in proof of the reality and truth of the justification sought. His argument is from the internal peace to the external peace. You have sought justification out of faith, he says; you have appropriated the sacrifice of Jesus Christ and His righteousness; you rest on Him, and interpose Him between you and God. Your conscience says, It is enough. For the first time you find satisfaction —your guilty fears subside and a sense of peace and exulting joy in the future prospect take their place. Is not this new-found satisfaction of conscience a proof of the reality of the justification you sought? This is Paul's argument.

But once more we need to pause and ask, How is the argument valid? External peace with God is inferred here from internal peace of conscience. What warrants such a tremendous inference? Is it so certain that because the qualms of our conscience are satisfied, therefore the demands of God's justice are satisfied? Here lies the deepest foundation of the argument; and it is important for us to realize fully this second of the implications which we have pointed out as necessarily lying at its basis. Its validity rests, as we have said, on the assumption that the human conscience is the shadow of God's judgment; that its deliverances repeat the demands of God's righteousness; and that its satisfaction, therefore, argues the satisfaction of God's justice.

But here again, tremendous as the assumption

is, we suppose it needs only to be clearly stated to be already accepted. For what is the question that is raised but, Whether the appeasing effect of Christ's blood of expiation is confined to the human conscience solely, while what we may call the divine conscience—God's sense of right—is left unaffected by it? And what is this question but this deeper one, Whether our moral sense is so out of analogy with God's moral sense that what fully meets and satisfies that moral indignation which rises in us on the realization of sin as sin, stands wholly out of relation with God's moral indignation at the spectacle of sin? Can this be a matter of doubt? Certainly it is to be hoped not. For so to affirm would obviously be to confound all our moral judgments. Not merely would it dethrone conscience from her empire over our lives and thoughts, but it would reduce unhappy man to a state far worse than that of the unreflecting brutes.

Far better to have no sense of right and wrong than to be cursed with a faculty as sensitive to moral distinctions as the needle is to the magnetic currents, and yet so wayward in its movements as to lead us continually astray, and bite back upon us with the bitterest remorse when perchance we have earned the praise of God. At the best, conscience would sink into the voice of hereditary custom; and what we call the right would be transmuted into the habitual, what has been found expedient in the present constitution of society. Its opposite would be equally right in a differently constituted social order—as Mr. Darwin tells us, indeed, affirming that were men organized according to the social order of, say, bees, what we fondly dream is the voice of God within us guarding the sacred boundary-lines that separate the domains of eternal right and wrong, would speak in opposite tones, requiring, with its categorical imperative, what it now brands as sin, and scourging us away from what we now look upon as right, with all its machinery of instinctive shrinking, sense of guilt, burning shame, and biting remorse.

Thus, as you will observe, all of what men call morality perishes out of the earth—the convenient and expedient take its place. And with it perishes also all that men call religion: for a God requiring we know not and cannot know what—who may be most deeply offended when we most sincerely strive to please Him—whose judgments of right and wrong are so out of analogy with ours that His most burning wrath may be stirred by our highest holiness, and His most gracious good pleasure evoked by what causes us the most agonizing regret, is clearly not a God whom such creatures as men may serve; nay, is clearly to us no God at all. The truth of our moral sense and blank atheism are the only alternatives. That men may remain men, as it is necessary that what they must believe to be true, is true; so it is necessary that what they must believe to be right, is right. The eternally ineradicable distinction of right and wrong, the changeless and sensitive truth of the human conscience to this distinction —these are the conditions, on the one hand, of human sanity; and the essential postulates, on the other, of all religion.

We need not fear to allow, therefore, that the validity of our sense of peace in the justification of faith rests on the correspondence between the moral sense of man and the moral sense of God. Without that correspondence no valid peace could ever, on any ground, visit the human heart. And a peace which is as deeply grounded as the reality of this correspondence, is rooted so profoundly in the nature of man that humanity itself must perish before that peace can be taken away. If there be a God at all, the author of our moral nature, it is just as certain as His existence that the moral judgment which He has implanted in us is true to the pole in the depths of His own moral being; that its deliverances as to right and wrong are but the transcripts of His own moral judgments; that it is rightly called the voice of God within us, and we may hearken to its decisions not so much with confidence that they will be confirmed in the forum of heaven as with the assurance that they are but the echoes of the divine judgment. We may confidently adopt, therefore, the strong language of Dr. Shedd, and say: "What, therefore, conscience affirms, in the transgressor's case, God affirms, and is the first to affirm. What, therefore, conscience feels in respect of the sinner's transgression, God feels, and is the first to feel. What, therefore, conscience requires in order that it may cease to punish the guilty spirit, God requires, and is the first to require. . . . The subjective in man is shaped by the objective in God, and not the objective in God by the subjective in man. The consciousness of the conscience is the reflex of the consciousness of God."

The sense of guilt by which the awakened conscience accuses us, speeding on into remorse, is thus perceived to be but the echo of God's judgment against sin. But this could not be if an appeased conscience were not the echo of God's judgment of justification. For, if conscience could cease to accuse while God continued to condemn, it would no longer be true that an accusing conscience is the sign of the condemnation of God, and a sense of guilt the reflex of His overhanging wrath. Conscience is, therefore, a mirror, placed in the human breast, upon which man may read the reflection of God's judgment upon his soul. When frowns of a just wrath conceal His face the clouds gather upon its polished surface; and surely when these clouds pass away, and the unclouded sun gleams upon us from the mirror, it cannot be other than the reflection of God's smile.

We seem now to have probed Paul's argument to the bottom. Man's conscience is but the reflection of God's judgment upon the soul. What satisfies man's conscience satisfies God's justice. The presentation to faith of an expiating and obedient Son of God, becoming man to take our place and stead before the law of God, and paying the penalty of our sin and keeping the probation due from us, satisfies the human conscience. The peace that steals into the heart of him who rests upon the Saviour in faith, and the joy that exults upon his lips as he contemplates the day when he shall stand in Him before the judgment seat of God—being but the rejoicing cry of the satisfied conscience—is to us the proof that God's wrath is really appeased, His condemnation reversed, and His face turned upon us in loving acceptance of us in His beloved Son. Surely, then, this experience of peace and joy is an irrefutable proof that this and no other is the just God's mode of justifying the sinner.

And now, men and brethren, what shall we do in the presence of these things? What but, first of all, follow the example of those old copyists who have transmitted to us the sacred text, and transmute Paul's appeal to the fact that Christians have peace and joy into an exhortation to ourselves to enter into this our peace and joy? By God's unspeakable grace the tidings of this gospel have come unto us. How Jesus Christ, who Himself was rich, has come into this poor world of ours that by His poverty we might be made rich—it has all been made known to us. And by God's superabounding grace in the Holy Spirit the ears of our hearts have been opened to the blessed proclamation. We have heard and believed. So, then, "having been justified by faith, let us have peace with God, through our Lord Jesus Christ, by whom also we have obtained access into this grace in which we stand;

and let us exult in the hope of the glory of God!"

Has the argument as we have probed it seemed long—too long for despairing feet to follow? Has its depth seemed too profound for the plummet of weak faith to sound? Blessed be God, it is not by following the argument of the apostle, by sounding the depths of his thought, that we are to enter into our peace; but by believing in Jesus Christ our Redeemer. We may drink at this fountain though we know not how the bubbling water forces its way to the surface—nor have time to investigate it, nor minds, mayhap, to comprehend it. Here is the water, and it is here to drink—living water—and whoso drinks of it shall never thirst, but it shall become in him a well of water springing up into eternal life. Let us thank God that He has not suspended our salvation on understanding; and even if we understand not, and our minds go halting as they strive to think His thoughts after Him, let us yet believe and enter into our peace.

And having once entered into our peace, let us turn and look with new eyes upon this life which we are living in the flesh. These difficulties, these dangers, these trials, these sufferings, how hard they have been to bear! We have deserved no better, but—nay, therefore—how hard they have been to bear! But we have been justified by faith—actually and truly justified by faith—and now we have peace with God. What a new aspect is taken by the trials and sufferings of life! They are no longer our fate, hard and grinding; they are no longer our punishment, better than which is not to be expected—for ever. They come from the hand of a reconciled God, from the hand of our Father. What one of them has not its meaning, its purpose, its freightage of mercy and of good? Shall we not follow the apostle here, and, as we find that peace with God has stolen into our hearts and that we are exulting in the hope of future glory, let that glory gild also our present pathway? Shall we not turn with new courage, nay, even with joy, to the sufferings of this present life, crying with him: "And not only so, but we also rejoice in tribulations, knowing that tribulation worketh patience, and patience triedness, and triedness hope, and hope putteth not to shame, because the love of God hath been shed abroad in our hearts through the Holy Spirit which was given unto us!"

What new light this is to shine on the weary pathway of God's saints! Says one of these saints, a follower of Paul in the sharpness of his afflictions as well as in the comfort he drew from them: "The Christian who lives not according to nature, but according to grace, should learn to give thanks to God *for all things* in Jesus Christ, as His holy and loving word commands us. And that is no more than right. For if we believe that when we were the enemies of God he gave His Son for us, to reconcile us to Himself, how should we not believe that all which He appoints for us *after that* not only comes not from His wrath, but comes really and literally from His love? And if God in afflicting us does not stop short at indifference, but goes the length of tenderness, is it not right that we in receiving our troubles should not stop short at patience, but go the length of thankfulness? As for myself," he adds, "in my short and scanty experience of the life of faith, I have often found that if resignation does not go so far as that, it does not give to our sufferings that sweetness which the Scripture promises." Here is the marvel of the Christian life. Not patience in afflictions merely, but thankfulness for them, says Adolph Monod, is our duty, nay, our privilege. Exult in joy over them, cries Paul; rejoice in them because we recognize in them but the "growing-pains" by which we are attaining "unto a full-grown man—

unto the measure of the stature of the fullness of Christ, that we may be no longer children, tossed to and fro and carried about with every wind of doctrine, by the sleight of man in craftiness, after the wiles of error; but dealing truly in love, may grow up *in all things* into Him which is the Head, even Christ."

And then the future! We used to look forward to it, perhaps, with nameless dread, with fearful expectation of judgment. What a glory has been thrown upon it by our new standpoint! We are no longer at enmity with God: we are at peace with God. Our conscience tells us that: we gaze on Christ and His sacrifice, and we know that God also sees it, and seeing it cannot condemn him who is in Christ. And when did Almighty God begin anything which He did not finish? And such a beginning! A beginning in indescribable, in inconceivable love. Our hearts are fairly dragged out of us in wondering love as we follow Paul's *a fortiori* argument. "For while we were yet weak, in due season Christ died for the ungodly. For scarcely for a righteous man will one die; yet perhaps for a good man some one would even dare to die. But God commendeth His love toward us, in that while we were yet sinners, Christ died for us. Much more then, being now justified by His blood, shall we be saved from wrath by Him. For if, while we were enemies, we were reconciled with God through the death of His Son, much more, being reconciled, shall we be saved by His life."

What means this peace in my heart? It means that the sense of guilt is allayed, that I am justified before God by the death of His dear Son. What means this justification with God? It means *much more*—that I shall be saved, by the life of His Son, from wrath. Much more! It is then much more than certain! Shall we not exult? Shall we not say with the apostle: " Much more being reconciled, shall we be saved by His life, and not only so, but also as those that rejoice in God through our Lord Jesus Christ, through whom we have now received this reconciliation"? Do we face the future now, then, with calmness? Ah, no! that would imply doubt. Do we face it, then, with courage? No; that would imply danger. Let us with the apostle face it with exultation, as becomes those who rejoice in God through our Lord Jesus Christ through whom we have *received* this reconciliation; as becomes those who, having been justified by faith, have peace with God, through Jesus Christ, and rejoice in the hope of the glory of God.

IV

THE PARADOX OF OMNIPOTENCE

IV

THE PARADOX OF OMNIPOTENCE

"All things are possible with God."—MARK x. 27 (R. V.).

OLIVER WENDELL HOLMES tells us that some ideas are so great that when they once find entrance into a human mind they permanently stretch it, and leave it for ever afterwards bigger. Surely this declaration of our Lord's embodies one of these mind-expanding ideas. For we must observe that its astounding declaration is not a mere hyperbole of careless speech, the negligent exaggeration of a proposition which has only relative validity. It is the well-weighed and precise assertion of a great fact. It does not mean merely that God is greater than man, and may accordingly be believed to be capable of doing some things which man cannot do. It means just what its startling words declare: that "all things"—taking the term in its unlimited absoluteness—that "all things are possible with God." Perhaps the conception is too large to find entrance into our minds at all. Perhaps none of us will fail to trim it down on this side or that in order to make it fit our several capacities of belief. But surely if it once gets into the mind, in the fullness of its meaning, it cannot fail permanently to enlarge it, to revolutionize all its points of view, and to raise it to a higher plane of both thought and feeling.

We may assure ourselves of the absoluteness of the meaning which our Lord intended to inject into the words by attending to the circumstances in which He announced them. The rich young ruler had come to Him, seeking eternal life; not with the simple-hearted trustfulness of a little child, nor yet with the self-despair of the publican who could only smite his breast and cry, "God be merciful to me, a sinner"; but, led by a rich man's instinct, with his thoughts bent on purchase. "Good Teacher," he asked, "what shall I do that I may inherit eternal life?" Jesus had probed his heart by setting a price on future blessedness which the young man was loath to pay: "Go, sell whatsoever thou hast, and give it to the poor; and come, follow Me." And when, with his countenance fallen, the young man had turned sorrowfully away, the great teacher improved the occasion for the instruction of His followers. "How hardly," he exclaimed, "shall they that have riches enter into the kingdom of God!" Perceiving the amazement of His disciples, He repeated the declaration, and this time, if we may trust the form in which the words have come to us in some of the oldest documents, in that universalized sense which is attached to them, in any event, in the sequel: "Children, how hard it is to enter into the kingdom of God!" And then, reverting for a moment to the specific case which was the occasion of the remark, and devoting Himself to driving home the impression which it was His prime object to make on their hearts, He gave utterance to that extraordinary comparison which has confounded the minds of His followers from that time until to-day: "It is easier for a camel to go through a needle's eye, than for a rich man to enter into the kingdom of God."

We all know how men have labored to rid this limitless assertion of the human impossibility of salvation of its necessary meaning. Some have thought to lessen at least the extremity of the affirmation by reading "cable" instead of "camel" —under the impression, apparently, that as a "cable" has some relation to the thread that would pass through a needle's eye, extreme difficulty might be expressed by it indeed, but not absurd impossibility. Others would have us believe that our Lord but "paltered here in a double sense," and had in mind not a real needle's eye, but some narrow gateway in Jerusalem, through which a camel could squeeze itself only with difficulty, and with the loss of whatever load it might essay to carry with it. All such emasculating interpretations, however, are shattered by our Lord's own explanation of His words. For when He observed His astonished disciples—who certainly understood Him to assert an unconditioned impossibility—asking wonderingly among themselves, "Who then can be saved?" He turned to them and said—what? "It is indeed difficult, but not impossible"? "I did but jest in ambiguous words; I meant, not an actual needle's eye, but that narrow passage you know of in Jerusalem"? No, but directly and emphatically this: "With men it *is* impossible."

It was an absolute impossibility He meant to affirm. Men can no more press themselves into the kingdom of heaven than a camel can force himself through a needle's eye. His solution of the paradox turns on no attenuation of the meaning the language is fitted to convey, but on a lofty appeal to the omnipotence of God. "With men it is impossible," he affirms; "but," he graciously adds, "not with God: for all things are possible with God." This special case of the impossible He meets by referring it to the general fact of the divine almightiness. This generalized enunciation of the divine almightiness is therefore to be taken in the height of its meaning. It is not to be weakened into the mere affirmation that God is very strong and can do things which man cannot understand. It is the ringing assertion of the true omnipotence of God. It is the grand announcement that the impossible constitutes the very sphere of the divine operation.

Nor have the followers of Jesus ever feared to take Him at His word. The heathen, the unbeliever, the infidel might scoff at the preachment, which has been to the Greeks of every age alike foolishness, and to the Jews a stumbling-block. But the offensive facts of this great gospel have ever been boldly proclaimed on the faith of a God to whom nothing is impossible. The incarnation, the redemption, the resurrection, the descent of the Spirit, regeneration, the entempling of God within the heart of man—these things may be pronounced by men preposterously impossible. Our fiery Tertullians have shown no wish to minimize their preposterous impossibility. They have rather drawn out in detail all the incredibilities, all the absurdities that may be thought to be inherent in them. Could the omnipotent God indeed be inclosed in a woman's womb? Could the infinite God really be pillowed on an earthly mother's breast? Could the omniscient God actually lisp in the prattle of a child? Could the self-existent One really die? The All-blessed hang a bruised and wounded sufferer upon the accursed cross? Do dead men ever rise again? Can they whose flesh has been dissolved in the corruption of the grave, take on again the firmness and freshness of youthful life? Can one who Himself died on a cross, between two thieves, be indeed the Life of the world? He who could not save Himself, can He really save others? Can a splash of water on the forehead wash away sin? Absurdities, impossibilities, enough! "I believe," cries Tertullian, "though they be impossible." And myriads have since boldly echoed his faithful cry.

Nay, the fervid old saint would turn the tables upon the objector. "I believe," he cries, "not merely *though* they be impossible: I believe *because* they are impossible!" For the impossible is the very sphere of God's activity; and we most readily credit the divine interposition in matters beyond the power of man. It is human to err: God's hand is seen when man waxes infallible. Man can slay: when dead men rise again we must needs perceive the finger of God. If water will not cleanse the soul, then it must be God who cleanses it in baptism. When those who are dead in trespasses and sins walk in newness of life we cannot choose but see displayed the power of God. Man's despair is indeed God's opportunity; and the things which are impossible to man are the very things which would be like God, which would be worthy of God, and which we should expect God to do. Tell me that God has left His throne to do what I am each day doing for myself, and what I am entirely competent to do for myself, and how can I believe? But tell me that God has descended from heaven to work what were impossible to His suffering creatures—then indeed I may believe the word. It is because man cannot save himself, that I may believe that God has intervened to save him. It is because man cannot cleanse his soul, that I can believe that God will interfere to cleanse it. It is because this world lies dead and corrupted in its sin, that I can believe that God will implant in it a germ of life which shall grow until it leavens the whole mass. It is because there are so many things impossible to poor puny man, that our hearts bound with joy at our Saviour's declaration that "all things are possible with God."

Now we must not fail to take very careful note that the matter which Jesus had in immediate mind when He made this great declaration was the salvation of the soul. "Good Teacher," was the young ruler's question, "what shall I do that I may inherit eternal life?" "Who then can be saved?" was the astounded question of the disciples, to which Jesus directly addressed His reply: "With men it is impossible, but not with God: for all things are possible with God." These words are, therefore, a direct assertion of the impossibility to man of salvation—of the "inheriting of eternal life," of "entering the kingdom of God," of "being saved," as it is variously called in the context—and the casting of man, therefore, for all his hope, on the God whose almighty power alone can do the impossible.

Speaking in theological language, here is then the sharpest possible enunciation of the doctrine of "inability." Man is unable to do anything that he may inherit eternal life, enter the kingdom of God, obtain salvation. These things are not merely difficult to him—to be done at all only at the cost of some great effort, some supreme expenditure of energy. They are impossible to him, as impossible as it is for a camel to go through the eye of a needle; and are, therefore, not to be done by him at all. An astonishing doctrine, men are accustomed to declare—rendering salvation hopeless to man. This, we must observe, is just what the disciples of Jesus said when He announced it to them. "And they were astonished exceedingly," we read, "saying among themselves, Then who can be saved?" We need not be surprised that a teaching which was a "hard saying" to the closest companions of Jesus still arouses hesitation in the minds of men. And our answer must still be the same which Jesus addressed to His astonished disciples; not an attempt to explain away the difficulty, not a minimizing of it, but a calm reiteration of the fact. "With men it *is* impossible."

Jesus does not stop here to tell us why it is impossible with men. He merely asseverates the fact. The incident which gave rise to His remarks and which determined their form may, indeed, help us a little way into the problem. Obviously the rich young man did not lack any human endowment. He had intellect to know the commandments of God; he had freedom of will to keep them; he had the moral sanity that comes from an upright life; he had the beauty of character that calls out the love of good men—"and Jesus," we are told, "looking upon him, loved him." Surely here is one, who, were it possible to man at all, might be expected to do what was necessary to inherit eternal life: one who, if any might, might well ask in some perplexity, "What lack I yet?" Nevertheless there was a fatal lack—not resident in his fundamental being as such by which he was a man, but in his ingrained disposition by which he was the man he was. And this prevented him from estimating at their true relative values the riches of this earth and the treasures in heaven; rendering it, as Jesus says, "impossible" for him to enter into the kingdom of God. And like him, every son of man, though possessed of treasures of knowledge and crowned with the most striking virtues, will be found to lack the power to put in their relatively proper places the things of God and the things of this world. With one it is riches, with another it is pride, with another it is ease, with another ambition, that has taken possession of the soul. With all there is real inability to rid themselves of "whatsoever they have" and turn single-heartedly to God.

If we probe deeply enough we shall find the root of this inability in sin—in a sin-distorted vision, feeling, judgment—in a word, in a sin-deformed soul, to which it is just as impossible "to be perfect" as it is for the lame leg not to limp or the misshapen pupil not to see awry. And therefore theologians are accustomed to say that the correct formula for human inability—while it certainly is not that man is unable to perform the right which he wills—just as certainly will not transmute the cannot into a mere will not, but will recognize a true inability even to will the right; a true inability rooted in a heart too corrupt to appreciate, desire or go out in an active inclination toward "the good." What is in itself corrupt cannot but be corrupted in all its activities.

Of all this, however, our Saviour says nothing in this context. It was not the uncovering to His disciples of the source of human inability in human sin to which He was here addressing Himself. He was occupying Himself entirely with the far more pressing task of detaching their hearts from trust in themselves and casting them upon God. Therefore He contents Himself with the emphatic assertion of the bare fact of human inability, and, fixing that with His pointed illustration well in their minds, directs them at once, in strong contrast, to the plenary ability of God. His sharp asseveration had wrought its work by arousing excessive astonishment in the minds of His hearers. The proof of its working came out in their wondering demand, "Then who can be saved?" No explanation follows: simply the calm reiteration of the astonishing declaration, "With men it *is* impossible." But therewith a call to them to raise their eyes, therefore, above man: "With men it *is* impossible, but *not with God: for all things are possible with God.*"

These words constitute, therefore, the core of the whole conversation. To them everything else had been leading up. And it was that He might assert them with due force and fix them in the hearts of His disciples with absolute firmness that everything else had been spoken. The great lesson that the Saviour was seeking to read His disciples was not that of human inability, but that of the divine ability. Human inability is dwelt upon only that in contrast with it the divine ability might be thrown out in strong emphasis. That man cannot save himself He would have them know; but the great truth on which He would have their minds rest was not that man cannot save himself, but that God can save him. Therefore everything is so ordered—incident and subsequent conversation alike—as to fix attention first on the helplessness of man, and then, by a powerful revulsion, to throw a tremendous emphasis on the almighty salvation of God. "With men it is impossible, but not with God: for all things are possible with God." Here, and here only, He would say, can you establish your feet, can you safely cast your hope.

It is almost impertinent to stop to admire the dialectic skill with which the desired impression is made. Our hearts cry out at once for the preciousness of the assurance that is given. We are men; and, like men, have been and are prone to think we can do "some good thing" by which we may earn eternal life. None know better than we how hard it is to be weaned from self-trust; how persistently we cherish the hope that thus, or thus, we may win for ourselves a title to bliss. But none know better than we the inevitable bitterness of the ensuing disappointment. It may be that, like the rich young ruler, we have kept the commandments from our youth up. It has not satisfied our hearts. We still are asking in unstilled longing, "What lack I yet? What good thing shall I do?" Nor is the longing ever thus satisfied. We may have piled Pelion on Ossa in our insatiable search after service. The ends of the earth may know our voice. And yet we may be pursued with the inextinguishable conviction that though we may preach to others we may yet ourselves be castaways. Though we may have bestowed all our goods to feed the poor, and though we may have even given our bodies to be burned, it profits us nothing. Still the cry rises in our soul, "What lack I yet? What good thing shall I do that I may have eternal life?"

We cannot still our craving with such things as these. Despair ever treads hard on hope, and the conviction is never shaken within us that by the work of the hands shall no flesh be justified. Earth's altars are the proof at once of the universal longing for salvation, and of the universal despair of salvation. No offering has been too precious to be immolated in expiation of sin; and none has been so precious as to take away the consciousness of sin. Else would they not have long since ceased to be offered? Least of all can we Christians, in whom the sense of sin has been quickened by the revelation of the righteously loving God in the face of Jesus Christ, ever still our hearts' despair with any deed of our own hands. If in times of forgetfulness we have been tempted to think well of ourselves and of our claims on God, it has required but a glance at Jesus and at our hearts in contrast with Him to awake us to a deeper sense of our unworthiness and helplessness. And when the veil is thus lifted, and we see ourselves in this true light, our temptation is not that we may hope to be saved without Him, but that we can scarcely hope to be saved with Him.

Let each of us to-day look within his own heart; let each of us permit to roll before the mind's eye the history of his soul's struggles—its hopes, its fears, its despairs. How much of it is a history of doubt, discouragement, and despondency! We know we cannot save ourselves. Our best efforts—have they not always ended in disillusionment? Our best hopes—have they not always gone out in failure? Our best determinations—have they not always sunk in gloom? Salvation—do we not ourselves know that it is impossible with men? Is it possible even with God? Then comes, like balm to our bruised hearts, our Lord's gracious assurance, "It *is* impossible with men, but not with God: for all things are possible with God." What an assurance! We are to trust in God for the salvation of our souls not because their salvation is easy. So soon as our eyes are open to what sin is, and to what God is, and to what we are, we know it is not easy. We are to trust in God for the salvation of our souls because He is one who does the impossible.

Do we clearly see that salvation is impossible to us, that a load of guilt rests upon us which we can never expiate? Our Saviour says, not that we are mistaken, not that if we will but try hard enough we may roll off the burden. No; He does not mock our despair. He fully recognizes the impossibility which our hearts have found. He says, " It *is* impossible with men, but not with God: for all things are possible with God." Thus He places the rock under our feet—the rock of the omnipotence of God. To nothing less than omnipotence can we trust to do this impossible thing. But we may well believe that there is no impossible to it. And resting on it our fretted souls may at last find peace.

It was, thus, that He might give us hope in the highest concerns that may awaken our anxieties, that our Lord enunciated in this startling manner the great fact of the divine omnipotence: " All things are possible with God." But the enunciation itself is quite general, and we should be wrong not to take comfort from the great truth here brought home to our hearts, in lesser affairs also. It is not so set forth as to suggest that it has no further application than that which Jesus gives it in this passage. On the contrary, this application is put forward as only a single instance under the general law. It is because "all things are possible with God" that we are bidden to be of good cheer with reference to eternal life, though to win it is obviously impossible with men. The fundamental proposition which our Lord emphasizes, therefore, is the broad and general declaration of the divine omnipotence. And He but teaches us how to take our practical comfort out of it when He applies it to calm our fears as to the possibility of salvation.

In how many other concerns of life do we need to find comfort in a similar application! We men are but puny creatures. We prate about being the architects of our own fortunes, the carvers of our own destinies, the masters of circumstance, who mold the world itself to our liking. We are but as children whistling to keep our courage up. There is none of us so young, so untried as not already to have learned that all things are not possible with men. In what bitter experiences this knowledge has come to us let each one's heart tell him to-day. Happy is he who has not been forced to learn it in wringings of soul and through blinding tears. We are set in this world in a vortex of forces. They beat, they seize upon us from every side; they whirl us this way and that, and drive us headlong often whither we would not. How often, when we would fain hew our passage through them, we stand blankly in the face of the impossible! How often, when the fight has been fought and the last possible blow has been struck, we stand aghast before obvious failure, and can but lift weak hands of prayer through the darkness up to God! Ah, it is in times like these that we may taste the sweetness of the great assurance of our Saviour: "All things are possible with God." How great, how inestimable a privilege to have the omnipotent God for our refuge!

And let us not fancy that the divine omnipotence is not available to us for such things as these: the grief that crushes our spirit, the failure that blackens our future, the disappointment that makes us at last see that the great design shall lie unfinished, and our lives be for ever incomplete. There is abroad among us far too much of a spurious spiritualism, which would look upon the common affairs of life, as it is pleased to call them—our human joys and hopes and fears and sorrows—as beneath the notice of God; and would steel our hearts in a Stoic's indifference to them. Our blessed Saviour's life among men rebukes so cold-hearted an attitude. He came burdened with the great task of the salvation of a world, but found no human pain and no human sorrow too trivial to pierce His heart with sympathetic pangs, too insignificant to call out His helping hand. "He went about doing good." No sick appealed to Him in vain, no weary came to Him without finding rest. He sighed over every human suffering; He wept with those who mourned; He bore the burdens of all. In His life He revealed the limitless breadth of the divine compassion which grieves with all the sorrows of men; and in His teaching He instructed us to flee to God for needed aid in every time of trouble.

The very hairs of our head, He told us, are all numbered, so that not one of them shall fall to the ground without His knowledge and permission. If in this world we are immersed in a perfect cyclone of forces, driving us this way and that, there is One ever by our side who shall be to us "as a hiding-place from the wind and a covert from the tempest." We may be weak, but He is strong; and He has bidden us to put our trust in Him, and promised that we shall not be made ashamed. On the omnipotence of God alone can we depend in the midst of the trials of this life as truly as for the hope of the life to come. And what gives the Christian his stability and peace in the strifes and conflicts of the world is naught else than that he feels beneath him the everlasting arms. It is only because he knows that the God to whom all things are possible rules in heaven and on earth, that he can commit his ways to Him, and be assured that all things shall indeed work together for good to those that love Him. The Christian's strength amid the evils of life is drawn from no lesser source than trust in the omnipotence of his God.

And all this has a very special application to the enheartening of those who have become fellow-workers with God in the salvation of the world. If disappointment and discouragement lie ever in wait for all who would fain do somewhat in the world, surely this is in a very especial sense true of those whose hearts are set upon the rescue of their fellow-men from the dominion of sin. He who would in any measure depend on an arm of flesh in this warfare is foredoomed to a very speedy despair. He may meet with little positive opposition or direct resistance. But oh, the dead weight of passive indifference which he will be sure to encounter! No wonder if the plaint of the prophet early becomes his own: "Lord, who hath believed our report, and to whom hath the arm of the Lord been revealed?" It will not be strange if he should experience periods of the deepest depression as he more and more realizes that he is crying into deaf ears and seeking to arouse to activity dead hearts. As the servant of the Lord God Almighty it will be strange, however, if he permits his natural sense of insufficiency to grow into a settled habit of despondency, and prosecutes his work under the shadow of an unhoping gloom. Let him, indeed, cry, "Lord, who is sufficient for these things?" Let him remember that even a Paul can do no more than plant, and even an Apollos can do no more than water. But let him remember also that the Lord both can and will give the increase: that the God whom he serves is the omnipotent God whose voice can wake even the dead, and that with Him "all things are possible."

And when we raise our eyes from the narrow circles of our own labors, and survey the progress of the gospel in the world, what shall we say then? Two thousand years have slipped away since Jesus laid the great commission upon the hearts of His people: " Go, disciple all the nations, . . . teaching them to observe all things whatsoever I commanded you!" We shall not permit ourselves to forget the enthusiasm, the splendid courage, the high hopes, the steadfast labor which many of His choicest servants have brought to the fulfillment of this commandment. Every land and clime has heard their cry and has been watered with their blood. Not least in our own day have the hosts of the Lord risen against the mighty; have His children flung themselves with a holy joy into the great task for which the Church exists. Yet the work still lags. As we stand to-day and survey the heathen world, how little seems accomplished! Surely we shall long since have concluded that the task is impossible —that no man and no body of men are really competent to turn the world upside down!

But we cannot give way to despair. As we come to know more fully the greatness of the masses of heathendom, and the depths into which they have sunk, and the ingrainedness of their points of view and inherited modes of thinking, we may indeed despair of men. We may readily enough perceive that no human power can avail to reverse the currents of centuries and to eradicate the evil habits of ages. But we cannot despair of God. "With men it is impossible," we may well say; but we must quickly add, "but not with God: for all things are possible with God." Resting on the divine omnipotence, we may well be sure that even this desert shall blossom like a rose, and may—not only in hope, but in firm expectation—await the fulfillment of the promises. And now, once occupying this position, how full the very air is of promise! Our eyes have seen the divine omnipotence at work, here and there, in the midst of the encircling gloom. Souls have been born again; Christian lives have shed a broad beam of light into the darkness; churches have been planted; Christian virtues have flourished where erstwhile only pagan vices were visible; the streaks of the dawn are appearing; the very air is palpitant with its prediction of the coming day. Our hope is set on the God who does great things without number. And this too will He in His own good time perform—for all things are possible with God.

Nor is the matter altered when we come nearer home and contemplate the heathen masses which crowd the narrow streets of our great cities. It is one of the signs of our times that the "slums," as we call them, have come forth to the observation of the world. And as they are brought more fully to public view the sight is not encouraging. Here the Christian worker comes to close quarters with vice and misery. Here his heart sinks within him at the manifest magnitude of the task that is set before him. Here he is gravely tempted to despair as he realizes more and more sharply the inadequacy of human methods and human powers to reach the root of the evil whose dreadful fruits daily smite him in the face. How easy it is to let the great hope die within us and seek to content ourselves with some lesser endeavor! This immense mass of corrupting humanity—we cannot lift it bodily to a higher plane. Shall we not be satisfied to attack the fringes of the evil, and be content with some less, indeed, but at least possible, accomplishment? There is, after all, we may say, only so much spiritual power in the world; why dissipate it in a Quixotic endeavor to reach the core of the evil, and not rather expend it wisely and warily in correcting at least some of its more menacing fruits? "There is, after all, only so much spiritual power in the world!" My brethren, it is an atheistic lie! The spiritual power in the world is the power of the omnipotent Jehovah. It does not waste with use; it does not recoil before the magnitude of any task. Rightly do you perceive such undertakings as these to be beyond the power of men: "with men they *are* impossible." But it is not so with God: "For all things are possible with God." Let us then face with fresh boldness this impossibility: there are no impossibilities with Him whose strength shall be in our right arm, mighty to tear down the strongholds of iniquity.

Ah, I know whither your hearts are wandering, my brethren! Yes, the blessed assurance is for this, too. Our battle with sin is not all with the sin that is without us. Christianity has come not only into the world, but into our hearts as well; and the promise of conquest over sin is not merely for the world, but also for our individual souls. Does the victory lag here also? Are we tempted from time to time to despair here too, as we are made to realize our proneness to evil, our ineradicable readiness to forget our good profession, lay down our arms, and give up the fight against temptation and transgression? Ah, who of us has not long since learned of the conquest over sin in the heart—that with men it is impossible? Let us learn also, with reference to it, too, that it is not so with God, "for all things are possible with God." I grant you that only He who does the impossible can cleanse the heart from its ingrained corruption, and can free the life from its continual sinning. But the God whom Jesus proclaims to us, in whom we may put our trust, is a God who does the impossible. And when we are tempted to despair, and are ready to yield the battle with the cry that it is impossible, let us raise our eyes to Him to whom there is no such thing as the impossible. And, believing His word, let us go on in His strength to the assured victory.

"O Lord God of Hosts,
Who is a mighty one like unto Thee,
O Jah?
And thy faithfulness is round about Thee!

* * * * * * *

Thou hast a mighty arm:
Strong is Thy hand, and high is Thy right hand.
Righteousness and judgment are the foundation of Thy throne:
Mercy and truth go before Thy face.
Blessed are the people that know the joyful sound:
That walk in the light of Thy countenance, O Lord!"

V

THE LOVE OF THE HOLY GHOST

V

THE LOVE OF THE HOLY GHOST

"Do ye think that the Scripture saith in vain, The spirit that dwelleth in us lusteth to envy?"—JAMES iv. 5. (A. V.)

THE translators have found some difficulty in rendering this verse. The form in which I have just read it, is that given it by our Authorized Version. I am not sure that it will at once convey the meaning. The Revised Version, in text and margin, presents several renderings. Among them there is one which expresses much more clearly what seems to me to be the meaning of the original. It is this: "Or think ye that the Scripture saith in vain, That Spirit which He made to dwell in us yearneth for us even unto jealous envy?" It is a declaration, on the basis of Old Testament teaching, of the deep yearning which the Holy Spirit, which God has caused to dwell in us, feels for our undivided and unwavering devotion.

In the context James had been speaking of the origin of the unseemly quarrels which even in that early day, it seems, marred the life of Christians. He traces them to greediness for the pleasures of this world, and consequent envy toward those who are better placed, or more fortunate in the pursuit of worldly goods. Then he turns suddenly to administer a sorrowful rebuke to the gross inconsistency of such envious rivalry in grasping after the pleasures of this world, for men who possess the inestimable treasure of God's love. It is at once observable on reading over the passage that its whole phraseology is colored by the underlying presentation of the relation of the Christian to God under the figure of marriage.

The Christian is the bride of God. And therefore any commerce with the world is unfaithfulness. There is not room in this relation for two loves. To love the world in any degree is a breach of our vows to our one husband, God. Hence the exclamation of "Adulteresses!" which springs to James' lips when he thinks of Christians loving the world. Hence his indignant outcry, "Know ye not that love of the world is enmity with God?" and his sweeping explanation, "Whosoever, therefore, has it in his mind to be a lover of the world is thereby constituted an enemy of God." We cannot have two husbands; and to the one husband to whom our vows are plighted, all our love is due. To dally with the thought of another lover is already unfaithfulness. On the other side, God is the husband of the Christian's soul. And He loves it with that peculiar, constant, changeless love with which one loves what the Scripture calls his own body (Eph. v. 28). Is the soul faithful to Him? Who can paint, then, the delight He takes in it? Is it unfaithful, turning to seek its pleasure in the love of the world? Then the Scripture tells us that it is with jealous yearning that God, its lawful husband, looks upon it. Does it, after unfaithfulness, turn again to its rightful lord? It cannot draw nearer to Him than He is ready to draw to it; and it no sooner humbles itself before Him than He exalts it.

The general meaning of the text is thus revealed to us as a strong asseveration of the love of God for His people, set forth under the figure of a faithful husband's yearning love for his erring bride. James presents this asseveration of God's love for His people, we will observe, as the teaching of Scripture; that is, since he was in the act of penning the earliest of New Testament books, as the teaching of the Old Testament Scriptures. The mode in which he makes this appeal to Scripture is perhaps worthy of incidental remark. "Or think ye that it is an empty saying of Scripture?" The question is a rhetorical one, and amounts to the strongest assertion that from James' point of view no saying of Scripture could be empty. He would confound his readers by adducing the tremendous authority of Scripture in support of his declaration; and therein he reveals to us the attitude of humble submission toward the Scripture word which characterizes all the writers of the New Testament.

It was not, however, the doctrine of inspiration which was then engaging his thought. He sends us to these inspired Scriptures rather for the doctrine of God's unchanging love toward His sinful people. And we will surely have no difficulty in recalling numerous Old Testament passages in which the Lord has been pleased graciously to express His love for His people under the figure of the love of a husband for his chosen bride; or in which He has been pleased to make vivid to us His sense of the injury done to His love by the unfaithfulness of His people, by attributing to Himself the burning jealousy of a loving husband toward the tenderly cherished wife who has wandered from the path of fidelity. Already this representation underlies expressions which occur in the Pentateuch, and indeed it is enshrined for us in the fabric of the Ten Commandments themselves, where God announces Himself as a jealous God who will visit the iniquities of the fathers upon the children, upon the third and upon the fourth generation of those that hate Him, while yet He shows mercy unto thousands of them that love Him and keep His commandments. In the later pages of the Old Testament psalmists vie with prophets in developing the figure in every detail of its application. Throughout all, the complaint of the Lord is: "Surely as a wife treacherously departeth from her husband, so have ye dealt treacherously with Me, O house of Israel, saith the Lord" (Jer. iii. 20). Throughout all, He pleads His changeless though outraged love for them. If He threatens that He will judge them as women that break wedlock are judged, and will bring upon them the blood of fury and jealousy (Ezek. xvi. 38), He adds: "Nevertheless I will remember My covenant with thee in the days of thy youth, and I will establish unto thee an everlasting covenant. Then shalt thou remember thy ways, and be ashamed . . . when I have forgiven thee all that thou hast done, saith the Lord God" (Ezek. xvi. 60–63). Throughout all, thus, there throbs the expression of that deep, appropriating love to which punishment is strange work, and which yearns to recover the fallen and restore them to favor and honor. Its hopes run forward in anticipation to that happy day when the wandering one shall listen once again to the alluring words of love spoken to her heart, and once more turn and call the Lord Ishi, "My husband." "And in that day," the Lord hastens to declare, "in that day will I make a covenant for them with the beasts of the field, and with the fowls of heaven, and with the creeping things of the ground: and I will break the bow and the sword and the battle out of the land, and will make them to lie down safely. And I will betroth thee unto Me for ever; yea I will betroth thee unto Me in righteousness, and in judgment, and in loving kindness, and in mercies. I will even betroth thee unto Me in faithfulness: and thou shalt know the Lord" (Hosea ii. 18–20).

In its general meaning, thus, our text is general Bible-teaching. It announces nothing which had not been the possession of God's people concerning His love for them from the days of old. Its message to us is just the common message of the whole Scripture revelation, in Old and New Testament alike. But it has its own peculiarities in expressing this one great common message of God's yearning love for His people. And possibly there may be found a special lesson for us in these peculiarities.

The first of them which claims our attention is the intense energy of the expression which is used here to declare the love of God for his erring people. He is said to "yearn for us, even unto jealous envy."

Modes of speech sufficiently strong had been employed in the prophets of the Old Testament, in the effort to communicate to men the vehemence of God's grief over their sin and the ardor of His longing to recover them to Himself. The simple attribution of the passion of jealousy to Him one would fancy a representation forcible enough. And this representation is heightened in every conceivable way. Even in Exodus (xxxiv. 14) we meet it in the strengthened form which declares that the very name of God is Jealous—" for the Lord, whose name is Jealous, is a jealous God"—as if this were the characteristic emotion which expressed His very being. Nahum tells us that "the Lord is a jealous God and avengeth; the Lord avengeth and is full of wrath" (Nahum i. 2). And in Zechariah we read that the Lord is "jealous for Zion with great jealousy, and He is jealous for her with great fury" (Zech. viii. 2).

But the language of James has an intensity which rises above all Old Testament precedent. Not only does the verb he uses express the idea of eager longing as strongly as it is possible to express it; but its already strong emphasis is still further enhanced by an adverbial addition which goes beyond all usage. The verb is that which is employed by the Greek translators of the Forty-second Psalm: "As the hart panteth after the water brooks, so panteth my soul after Thee, O God." So, with the thirst of the famishing hart for water—so, says James, does God pant after His people whose minds wander from Him. The adverb is one which often occurs in the classics to express the feeling which one is apt to cherish toward a rival; but it is not the ordinary active word for jealousy which is frequently elsewhere applied to God in the Scriptures, but a term of deeper passion which is never elsewhere applied to God, and which is expressive rather of the envious emotion which tears the soul as it contemplates a rival's success. So, with this sickening envy, says James, God contemplates our dallying with the world and the world's pleasures. He envies the world our love—the love due to Him, pledged to Him, but basely withdrawn from Him and squandered upon the world. The combined expression is, you will see, astonishingly intense. God is represented as panting, yearning, after us, even unto not merely jealousy, but jealous envy. Such vehemence of feeling in God is almost incredible; and some commentators, indeed, refuse to believe that it can be ascribed to Him and declare the anthropomorphism involved to be altogether too extreme.

Let us not, however, refuse the blessed assurance that is given us. It is no doubt hard to believe that God loves us. It is doubtless harder to believe that He loves us with so ardent a love as is here described. But He says that He does. He declares that when we wander from Him and our duty toward Him, He yearns after us and earnestly longs for our return; that He envies the world our love and would fain have it turned back to Himself. What can we do but admiringly cry, Oh, the breadth and length and height and depth of the love of God which passes knowledge! There is no language in use among men which is strong enough to portray it. Strain the capacity of words to the utmost and still they fall short of expressing the jealous envy with which He contemplates the love of His people for the world, the yearning desire which possesses Him to turn them back to their duty to Him. It is this inexpressibly precious assurance which the text gives us; let us, without doubting, embrace it with hearty faith.

Another peculiarity of the text lies in the clearness with which it distributes the object of this great love of God into individuals.

When the Scriptures make use of the figure of marriage to reveal God's love to His people, it is commonly His people as a body which they have in mind. It is, in the Old Testament, the "house of Israel" whom Jehovah has chosen to be His wife; in the New Testament it is the church which is the bride, the Lamb's wife. Individuals, as members in particular of the body of Israel or of the church, partake of its fortunes, share in the love poured out upon it, and contribute by their lives to the foulness of its sin or to the beauty of its holiness. It is only as the members are holy that the church can be that glorious church, not having spot or wrinkle or any such thing, but holy and without blemish, which Christ is to present to Himself at the last day. But, though the individuals thus share in the love and glory of the church, it is the church itself and not the individual which is prevailingly represented as the bride of the Lamb. Only occasionally, in the application of the figure, do the individuals seem to be prominently in mind (Ps. lxxiii. 27; Rom. vii. 4).

In our present passage, however, the reference is directed to the individual and not to the church as a body. It is the individual Christian who is in covenant vows to God, and who is forgetting these vows, when in the prosecution of his pleasures he strives and fights his fellow-man, instead of depending on God's love to fulfill all his wants. It is the individual who is warned that he is guilty of spiritual adultery when he permits the least shade of love of the world to enter his heart; and that the cherishing of such love even in thought is an act of enmity against God. It is the individual who is assured that God jealously envies the world the love which He gives it, and yearns after the return of His love to Him, the Lord, who "longeth for him even unto jealous envy."

This clear individualization of the great truth which the passage enshrines is surely fraught with a very precious message to us. Not the church merely—we might believe that, knowing ourselves only as unworthy members of what is in idea a glorious church: not the church merely, but you and I are, each, declared to be covenanted with the Lord in the bonds of this holy and intimate relationship, the recipients of His loving care as His bride, nay, the objects of His changeless and yearning affection. Surely this too is an inexpressibly precious assurance, which we would fain, without doubting, embrace with hearty faith.

A third peculiarity of the text lies in its direct attribution of this appropriating love of God for His chosen ones to God the Holy Spirit.

In this the text is almost unique in the whole range of Scripture. In the Old Testament it is Jehovah, the covenant God, who represents the covenanted union between Israel and Himself under the figure of a marriage. It is Jehovah whose name is Jealous; and whose jealousy burns unto envy as he contemplates the unfaithfulness of Israel. In the New Testament it is prevailingly Christ, the Lamb, who has taken the Church unto Himself as His bride; and who loves and cherishes His Church as a husband loves and cherishes his wife. But in our present passage it is specifically God the Holy Spirit who is represented as the subject of this envious jealousy and this yearning affection. "Or think ye that it is a vain and empty saying of Scripture, that the Spirit which He made to dwell in us yearneth jealously?"

And surely it is a great gain from the point of view of the Christian life to have this explicit revelation of the heart of the indwelling Spirit. What James tells us is that it is God the Holy Spirit, whom God has caused to dwell within us, who is the subject of the unchanging love of God's people which is expressed in these words of unexampled strength, as a yearning after us even to jealous envy. Surely this too is an inexpressibly precious assurance which we would fain, without doubting, embrace with hearty faith.

And now let us try to realize, in the simplest possible way, what is involved for us in this precious assurance.

Primarily, then, as we have seen, James makes known to us here the precious fact that the Holy Spirit loves us.

It is easy to say that this is so far from being a new fact to which the Christian consciousness is unwonted, that it is necessarily implicated in the fundamental Christian postulate that God is love. As the Godhead is one and cannot be divided, so each person of the Godhead must be the love that God is. The Father is no more love, and the Son is no more love, than the Spirit is love; and when we confess that God is love, we confess by necessary implication that the Holy Spirit, who is God, is Himself love. But it will be far more to the point for us to ask ourselves in all seriousness if we have been in the habit of realizing to ourselves the blessed fact that the Holy Spirit loves us. This does not seem to be a form of gratulation in which Christians are accustomed to felicitate themselves.

Our prayers, our jubilations, thank God, also our hearts, are full of the precious facts that the Father loves us and the Son loves us. " For God so loved the world, that He gave His only begotten Son, that whosoever believeth on Him should not perish, but have eternal life." " Behold what manner of love the Father hath bestowed upon us, that we should be called children of God." "Herein is love, not that we loved God, but that He loved us, and sent His Son to be the propitiation for our sins." " God commendeth His own love toward us, in that, while we were yet sinners, Christ died for us." " God, being rich in mercy, for His great love wherewith He loved us, even when we were dead through our trespasses, quickened us together with Christ." "The love of Christ which passeth knowledge." "Christ also loved you and gave Himself up for us an offering and a sacrifice to God." "Hereby know we love, because He laid down His life for us." "Greater love hath no man than this, that a man lay down his life for his friends." "Who shall separate us from the love of Christ?" It is in such texts as these that the Christian soul finds the heavenly manna, on which it feeds and grows strong. It is with these glorious truths—that God the Father loves us, that Christ the Saviour loves us—that we comfort one another in times of darkness and trial; it is these glorious truths that we whisper to our own souls in their moments of weakness and dismay. We never let them escape us. We dare never let them escape us. For to lose hold of them is to feel the light fade from life and the dense darkness of hopeless agony settle down on the heart.

But do we so constantly remember that the Holy Spirit loves us? Do we comfort ourselves so often and so fully with this great fact? We feel the lift of John's appeal: "Beloved, if God so loved us, we also ought to love one another." We feel the force of Paul's declaration that "the love of Christ constraineth us." But do we feel equally the force of Paul's similar appeal: "Now I beseech you, brethren, by the love of the Spirit, that you strive together with me in your prayers to God"? Are we equally impelled to a life of single-hearted devotion to God by James' challenge: "Or think ye that it is a vain and empty saying of Scripture, that the Spirit which God hath made to dwell in us yearneth after us even unto jealous envy"? Oh, does it not too often pass over our minds as if it were really a vain and empty saying? The love of the Spirit! The yearning, jealous love of the Holy Ghost for our souls! May it come to mean much to us and be ever in our hearts to strengthen and comfort them.

Doubtless the comparative infrequency with which we meditate upon the love which the Holy Ghost bears to us is due partly to the infrequency with which the love of the Spirit is expressly mentioned in Scripture. It is also, however, due partly, doubtless, to our not habitually connecting in our minds the work of the Holy Spirit in the salvation of men with its motive in His ineffable love for us.

We ascribe to God, the Father, the plan of salvation; and to God, the Son, the impetration of redemption under that plan; and to God, the Holy Ghost, the application to the souls of sinners of the redemption procured by the Son. We recognize the necessity of the office-work of each person of the blessed Trinity if souls are to be saved. And, if we face the point now and then, we recognize that each step in the blessed progress of salvation is equally the pure outflow of the incredible love of God—the striving of the Holy Ghost with the sinner in bringing salvation to fruition in the heart, no less than the humiliation of the Son of God even unto the death of the cross, or the gift by the Father of His only begotten to suffer and die for a lost world. But we are accustomed in our thought of it to connect the saving work of the Father and the Son with the love which dictated it. We are accustomed to say to ourselves with never ceasing wonder that "God so loved the world, that He gave His only begotten Son," that "greater love hath no man than this, that a man lay down his life for his friends." And we, perhaps, are not so much accustomed to connect in thought the saving work of the Holy Spirit with the love which no less dictated it. We are, perhaps, not so much accustomed to say to ourselves that herein is love manifested, that the Spirit of all holiness is willing to visit such polluted hearts as ours, and even to dwell in them, to make them His home, to work ceaselessly and patiently with them, gradually wooing them—through many groanings and many trials—to slow and tentative efforts toward good; and never leaving them until, through His constant grace, they have been won entirely to put off the old man and put on the new man and to stand new creatures before the face of their Father God and their Redeemer Christ. Surely herein is love! But we are perhaps too little accustomed to remind ourselves explicitly of it.

Yet what immense riches of comfort and joy this great truth has in it for our souls! Were the work of the application of Christ's redemption to us performed by some mere servant-agent, indifferent to us, and intent only on perfunctorily fulfilling the task committed to him, we might well tremble for our salvation. We know our hearts. We know how sluggish they are in yielding to the drawings of the Spirit. We know how slow they are to forsake sin; how determined they are to cling to their darling iniquities. Ah, well may James declare that our pleasures have taken up arms and pitched their camps in our members, ready for "war to the knife," as we say, with every good impulse; and Paul, in like manner, that the law in our members arrays itself in war against the new desires implanted in the mind by the Spirit, so that in view of this condition he is impelled to cry out, O wretched man that I am, who shall deliver us from the body of this death! Surely the heart of every one of us has often echoed that cry of natural despair. Were these hearts of ours committed to the molding of one who wrought with us only under a sense of duty and not as upheld by untiring love toward us, what hope of the issue could we cherish? There is no possible deed of ingratitude, opposition, rejection toward the Spirit's work in us of which we have not been guilty. Can we hope that He will bear with us? It is only such love that He cherishes toward us—the model of that love which Paul so sympathetically describes, that suffereth long, is not provoked, beareth all things, hopeth all things, believeth all things, endureth all things—that could possibly outlive our shameful disregard and our terrible backsliding. It is only because the Spirit which He hath caused to dwell in us yearneth for us even unto jealous envy, that He is able to continue His gracious work of drawing our souls to God amid the incredible oppositions which we give to His holy work.

And here we must not omit to take particular notice of another aspect of the same great fact, as James brings it before us. Observe how he here designates the Spirit, whose great love he has portrayed. It is as the "Spirit whom God has caused to dwell within us." It is He, the indwelling Spirit, who, we are told, yearns for us with envious jealousy whenever the world obtains a hold upon our hearts.

God in heaven loves us; and it is because God in heaven loves us that He has given His Son to die for us. Christ on the cross—nay, rather, Christ who once hung on the cross, but is now seated at the right hand of God, a Prince and a Saviour—loves us; and it is because Christ loves us that He died for us, and is now become head over all things for His Church, that all things may work together for good to those who love Him. But the Spirit in our hearts also loves us. Infinite love is above us; infinite love is around us; and, praise be to God! infinite love dwells in us. See how close the love of God is brought to us. It is made to throb in our very hearts; to be shed abroad within us; and to work subtly upon us, drawing us to itself, from within.

In the light of this great truth we may perhaps better understand the meaning of Paul when, depicting the conflict going on within the heart of the newborn man, he declares that the flesh lusteth against the Spirit, and the Spirit against the flesh, as if the Spirit were part of our very being—the only part of our being which lusts against evil, "that we may not do the things that we would." And again in its light, we may perhaps understand somewhat better that other great passage in which Paul declares that when we pray the Holy Spirit maketh intercession for us with groanings which cannot be uttered. Our prayers may be feeble because our hatred against sin is weak. But there is One within us, who loves us with an imperishable love and hates sin with a perfect hatred; and His groans of longing for our release from the bondage of sin reinforce our weak cries. His unutterable groans for us sinners are the measure of His unutterable love for us sinners.

And let us not fail to gather the full gracious meaning of the word "dwell" here. It is the word to denote permanent habitation in contradistinction from temporary sojourning. God has caused the Spirit of love not to visit our hearts merely, but to abide there; not to tarry there for a season merely, tentatively, as it were, and on trial, but to make His home there, to "settle" there, to establish His permanent dwelling there. "Think ye," asks James, "that it is a vain and empty saying of Scripture, that the Spirit which God hath caused to settle permanently in our hearts as His home, yearneth after us with jealous envy?"

Ah, when God has covenanted with the soul, it is with no half-heartedness! When He represents Himself as having taken us to Himself as a husband takes a wife in the bonds of a holy covenant, it is no temporary union which He has in mind. He leaves no prudent way of escape open to Himself. With Him the covenant is for ever. He sends the Spirit into our hearts—to make His home there. And it is because, on His part, the covenant is an eternal covenant, and He takes up His abode within us for ever, that, when we treat it with levity and lightly break its bonds, He yearneth after us with jealous envy, and cannot be content until He has won us absolutely back to Himself and has eradicated from our hearts every particle of longing for the world and its sinful pleasures. What a great, what an enheartening truth we have here! God dwells within us, dwells there permanently, and this indwelling God loves us, loves us with such changeless love that even our insults to His love are met by Him only with yearning after us even unto jealous envy.

How deeply we are touched by the stories which reach us from time to time of the persistent love of a father for a wandering son, or of a brother for a sinful brother, or of a friend for a friend who has fallen into evil courses; of how it follows the reckless sinner into all his wicked associations, enters the saloon with him, the gambling hell, the brothel; argues, pleads, uses kindly violence, seeks every mode of restoration possible with unwearied patience and persistency, is not cast off by curses or by blows, or by any evil entreatment, but pursues with constancy and unfailing tact and tender perseverance its one changeless purpose of rescue. Here is the faint reflection of the Holy Spirit's love for our souls.

See us steeped in the sin of the world; loving evil for evil's sake, hating God and all that God stands for, ever seeking to drain deeper and deeper the cup of our sinful indulgence. The Spirit follows us unwaveringly through all. He is not driven away because we are sinners. He comes to us because, being sinners, we need Him. He is not cast off because we reject His loving offices. He abides with us because our rejection of Him would leave us helpless. He does not condition His further help upon our recognizing and returning His love. His continuance with us is conditioned only on His own love for us. And that love for us is so strong, so mighty, and so constant that it can never fail. When He sees us immersed in sin and rushing headlong to destruction, He does not turn from us, He yearns for us with jealous envy.

It is in the hands of such love that we have fallen. And it is because we have fallen into the hands of such love that we have before us a future of eternal hope. When we lose hope in ourselves, when the present becomes dark and the future black before us, when effort after effort has issued only in disheartening failure, and our sin looms big before our despairing eyes; when our hearts hate and despise themselves, and we remember that God is greater than our hearts and cannot abide the least iniquity; the Spirit whom He has sent to bring us to Him still labors with us, not in indifference or hatred, but in pitying love. Yea, His love burns all the stronger because

THE LOVE OF THE HOLY GHOST

we so deeply need His help: He is yearning after us with jealous envy.

Among the legends which popular fancy has woven around the memory of Francis of Assisi, we are told that he was riding along one day in the first joy of his new-found peace, his mind possessed with a desire to live over again the life of absolute love which his Divine master had lived in the earth. Suddenly, "at a turn in the road, he found himself face to face with a leper. The frightful malady had always inspired in him an invincible repulsion. He could not control a movement of horror, and by instinct he turned his horse in another direction." Then came the quick revulsion of feeling. "He retraced his steps and, springing from his horse, he gave to the astounded sufferer all the money that he had; and then kissed his hand, as he would have done to a priest." A new era in his spiritual life had dawned. He visited the lazaretto itself and with largesses of alms and kindly words sought to bring some brightness of the outside world into that gloomy retreat. Still his love grew stronger. The day came when he made the great renunciation and stood before men endued with naught but the love of Christ. Now no temporary lazaretto contented him. He must dwell there as a permanent sunbeam to the distressed. He came now with empty hands, but with a heart full to overflowing with compassion. "Taking up his abode in the midst of the afflicted he lavished upon them a most touching care, washing and wiping their sores, all the more gentle and radiant as the sores were more repulsive."

It is not given to man, of course, even to comprehend, much less to embody in a legend like this, all the richness of God's mysterious love for sinners. But in such legends as this we may catch some faint shadow of what the Spirit's love for us means. No leprous sores can be as foul in the eyes of the daintiest bred as sin is foul in the eyes of the Holy Ghost. We cannot conceive of the energy of His shrinking from its polluting touch. Yet He comes into the foul lazaretto of our hearts and dwells there—permanently lives there; not for Himself, or for any good to accrue to Himself; but solely that He may cleanse us and fit us to be what He has made us, the Bride, the Lamb's wife.

Could there be presented to us a more complete manifestation of the infinite love of God than is contained in this revelation of the love of the Spirit for us? God is love. Does not this greatest of all revelations take on a new brightness and a new force to move our souls when we come to realize that not only is the Father love, and the Son love, but the Spirit also is love; and so wholly love that, despite the foulness of our sin, He yearneth for us even unto jealous envy?

Could there be given us a higher incentive to faithfulness to God than is contained in this revelation of the love of the Spirit for us? Are our hearts so hard that they are incapable of responding to the appeal of such a love as this? Can we dally with the world, seek our own pleasures, forget our duty of love to God, when the Spirit which He hath made to dwell in us is yearning after us even unto jealous envy?

Could there be afforded us a deeper ground of encouragement in our Christian life than is contained in this revelation of the love of the Spirit for us? Is hope so dead within us that it is no longer possible for us to rest with confidence upon such love? Can we doubt what the end shall be—despite all that the world can do to destroy us, and the flesh and the devil—when we know that the Spirit which He hath made to dwell in us is yearning after us even unto jealous envy?

Could there, then, be granted us a firmer foundation for the holy joy of Christian assurance than is contained in this revelation of the love of the Spirit for us? Is faith grown so weak that it cannot stay itself on the almighty arm of God? Surely, surely, though our hearts faint within us, and the way seems dark, and there are lions roaring in the path, we shall be able to look past them all to the open gates of pearl beyond, whensoever we remember that the Spirit which He hath made to dwell within us is yearning after us even unto jealous envy!

VI

THE LEADING OF THE SPIRIT

VI

THE LEADING OF THE SPIRIT

"For as many as are led by the Spirit of God, these are sons of God."—ROM. viii. 14. (R. V.)

THESE words constitute the classical passage in the New Testament on the great subject of the "leading of the Holy Spirit." They stand, indeed, almost without strict parallel in the New Testament. We read, no doubt, in that great discourse of our Lord's which John has preserved for us, in which, as He was about to leave His disciples, He comforts their hearts with the promise of the Spirit, that "when He, the Spirit of truth, is come, He shall guide you into all the truth." But this " guidance into truth " by the Holy Spirit is something very different from the "leading of the Spirit" spoken of in our present text; and it is appropriately expressed by a different term. We read also in Luke's account of our Lord's temptation that He was "led by the Spirit in the wilderness during forty days, being tempted of the devil," where our own term is used. But though undoubtedly this passage throws light upon the mode of the Spirit's operation described in our text, it can scarcely be looked upon as a parallel passage to it. The only other passage, indeed, which speaks distinctly of the "leading of the Spirit" in the sense of our text is Gal. v. 18, where in a context very closely similar Paul again employs the same phrase: "But if ye are led by the Spirit, ye are not under the law." It is from these two passages primarily that we must obtain our conception of what the Scriptures mean by "the leading of the Holy Spirit."

There is certainly abundant reason why we should seek to learn what the Scriptures mean by "spiritual leading." There are few subjects so intimately related to the Christian life, of which Christians appear to have formed, in general, conceptions so inadequate, where they are not even positively erroneous. The sober-minded seem often to look upon it as a mystery into which it would be well not to inquire too closely. And we can scarcely expect those who are not gifted with sobriety to guide us in such a matter into the pure truth of God. The consequence is that the very phrase, "the leading of the Spirit," has come to bear, to many, a flavor of fanaticism.

Many of the best Christians would shrink with something like distaste from affirming themselves to be "led by the Spirit of God"; and would receive with suspicion such an averment on the part of others, as indicatory of an unbalanced religious mind. It is one of the saddest effects of extravagance in spiritual claims that, in reaction from them, the simple-minded people of God are often deterred from entering into their privileges. It is surely enough, however, to recall us to a careful searching of Scripture in order to learn what it is to be "led by the Spirit of God," simply to read the solemn words of our text: "As many as are led by the Spirit of God, these are sons of God." If the case be so, surely it behooves all who would fain believe themselves to be God's children to know what the leading of the Spirit is.

Let us, then, commit ourselves to the teaching of Paul, and seek to learn from him what is the meaning of this high privilege. And may the Spirit of truth here too be with us and guide us into the truth.

Approaching the text in this serious mood, the first thing that strikes us is that the leading of the Spirit of God of which it speaks is not something peculiar to eminent saints, but something common to all God's children, the universal possession of the people of God.

"As many as are led by the Spirit of God," says the apostle, "these are sons of God." We have here in effect a definition of the sons of God. The primary purpose of the sentence is not, indeed, to give this definition. But the statement is so framed as to equate its two members, and even to throw a stress upon the coextensiveness of the two designations. "As many as are led by the Spirit of God, these and these only are sons of God." Thus, the leading of the Spirit is presented as the very characteristic of the children of God. This is what differentiates them from all others. All who are led by the Spirit of God are thereby constituted the sons of God; and none can claim the high title of sons of God who are not led by the Spirit of God. The leading of the Spirit thus appears as the constitutive fact of sonship. And we dare not deny that we are led by God's Spirit lest we therewith repudiate our part in the hopes of a Christian life. In this aspect of it our text is the exact parallel of the immediately preceding declaration, which it thus takes up and repeats: "But if any one hath not the Spirit of Christ, that one is not His."

It is obviously a mistake, therefore, to look upon the claim to be led by God's Spirit as an evidence of spiritual pride. It is rather a mark of spiritual humility. This leading of the Spirit is not some peculiar gift reserved for special sanctity and granted as the reward of high merit alone. It is the common gift poured out on all God's children to meet their common need, and is the evidence, therefore, of their common weakness and their common unworthiness. It is not the reward of special spiritual attainment; it is the condition of all spiritual attainment. In its absence we should remain hopelessly the children of the devil; by its presence alone are we constituted the children of God. It is only because of the Spirit of God shed abroad in our hearts that we are able to cry, Abba, Father.

We observe, therefore, next that the end in view in the spiritual leading of which Paul speaks is not to enable us to escape the difficulties, dangers, trials or sufferings of this life, but specifically to enable us to conquer sin.

Had the former been its object, it might indeed have been a special grace granted to a select few of God's children, and its possession might have separated them from among their brethren as the peculiar favorites of the Deity. Since, however, the latter is its object, it is the appropriate gift of all those who are sinners, and is the condition of their conquest over the least of their sins. In the preceding context Paul discovers to us our inherent sin in all its festering rottenness. But he discovers to us also the Spirit of God as dwelling in us and forming the principle of a new life. It is by the presence of the Spirit within us alone that the bondage in which we are by nature held to sin is broken; that we are emancipated from sin and are no longer debtors to live according to the flesh. This new principle of life reveals itself in our consciousness as a power claiming regulative influence over our actions; leading us, in a word, into holiness.

If we consider our life of new obedience from the point of view of our own activities, we may speak of ourselves as fighting the good fight of faith; a deeper view reveals it as the work of God in us by His Spirit. When we consider this Divine work within our souls with reference to the end of the whole process we call it sanctification; when we consider it with reference to the process itself, as we struggle on day by day in the somewhat devious and always thorny pathway of life, we call it spiritual leading. Thus the "leading of the Holy Spirit" is revealed to us as simply a synonym for sanctification when looked at from the point of view of the pathway itself, through which we are led by the Spirit as we more and more advance toward that conformity to the image of His Son, which God has placed before us as our great goal.

It is obvious at once then how grossly it is misconceived when it is looked upon as a peculiar guidance granted by God to His eminent servants in order to insure their worldly safety, worldly comfort, even worldly profit. The leading of the Holy Spirit is always for good; but it is not for all goods, but specifically for spiritual and eternal good. I do not say that the good man may not, by virtue of his very goodness, be saved from many of the sufferings of this life and from many of the failures of this life. How many of the evils and trials of life are rooted in specific sins we can never know. How often even failure in business may be traced directly to lack of business integrity rather than to pressure of circumstances or business incompetency is mercifully hidden from us. Nor do I say that the gracious Lord has no care for the secular life of His people. But it surely is obvious that the leading of the Spirit spoken of in the text is not in order to guide men into secular goods; and it is not to be inferred to be absent when trials come—sufferings, losses, despair of this world. It is specifically in order to guide them into eternal good; to make them not prosperous, not free from care or suffering, but holy, free from sin. It is not given us to save us from the consequences of our business carelessnesses or incompetences, to take the place of ordinary prudence in the conduct of our affairs. It is not given us to preserve us from the necessity of strenuous preparation for the tasks before us or from the trouble of rendering decision in the difficult crises of life. It is given specifically to save us from sinning; to lead us in the paths of holiness and truth.

Accordingly, we observe next that the spiritual leading of which Paul speaks is not something sporadic, given only on occasion of some special need of supernatural direction, but something continuous, affecting all the operations of a Christian man's activities throughout every moment of his life.

It has but one end in view, the saving from sin, the leading into holiness; but it affects every single activity of every kind—physical, intellectual, and spiritual—bending it toward that end. Were it directed toward other ends, we might indeed expect it to be more sporadic. Were it simply the omniscence of God placed at the disposal of His favorites, which they might avail themselves of in times of perplexity and doubt, it might well be occasional and temporary. But since it is nothing other than the power of God unto salvation, it must needs abide with the sinner, work constantly upon him, enter into all his acts, condition all his doings, and lead him thus steadily onward toward the one great goal.

It is easy to estimate, then, what a perversion it is of the "leading of the Spirit" when this great saving energy of God, working continually in the sinner, is forgotten, and the name is accorded to some fancied sporadic supernatural direction in the common offices of life. Let us not forget, indeed, the reality of providential guidance, or imagine that God's greatness makes Him careless of the least concerns of His children. But let us much more not forget that the great evil under which we are suffering is sin, and that the great promise which has been given us is that we shall not be left to wander, self-directed, in the paths of sin into which our feet have strayed, but that the Spirit of holiness shall dwell within us, breaking our bondage and leading us into that other pathway of good works, which God has afore prepared that we should walk in them.

All of this will be powerfully supported and the subject perhaps somewhat further elucidated if we will seek now to penetrate a little deeper into the inmost nature of the work of the Holy Spirit which Paul calls here a "leading," by attending more closely to the term which he has chosen to designate it when he calls it by this name. This term, as those skilled in such things tell us, is one which throws emphasis on three matters: on the extraneousness of the influence under which the movement suggested takes place; on the completeness of the control which this influence exerts over the action of the subject led; and on the pathway over which the resultant progress is made. Let us glance at each of these matters in turn.

One is not led when he goes his own way. It is only when an influence distinct from ourselves determines our movements that we can properly be said to be led. When Paul, therefore, declares that the sons of God are "led by the Spirit of God," he emphasizes, first of all, the distinction between the leading Spirit and the led sons of

God. As much as this he declares with great emphasis—that there is a power within us, not ourselves, that makes for righteousness. And he identifies this extraneous power with the Spirit of God. The whole preceding context accentuates this distinction, inasmuch as its entire drift is to paint the conflict which is going on within us between our native impulses which make for sin, and the intruded power which makes for righteousness. Before all else, then, spiritual leading consists in an influence over our actions of a power which is not to be identified with ourselves —either as by nature or as renewed—but which is declared by the apostle Paul to be none other than the Spirit of God Himself.

We thoroughly misconceive it, therefore, if we think of spiritual leading as only a conquest of our lower impulses by our higher nature, or even as a conquest by our regenerated nature of the remnants of the old man lingering in our members. Both of these conquests are realities of the Christian life. The child of God will never be content to be the slave of his lower impulses, but will ever strive, and with ultimate success, to live on the plane of his higher endowments. The regenerated soul will never abide the remnants of sin that vex his members, but will have no rest until he eradicates them to the last shred. But these victories of our nobler selves—natural or gracious—over what is unworthy within us, do not so much constitute the essence of spiritual leading as they are to be counted among its fruits. Spiritual leading itself is not a leading of ourselves by ourselves, but a leading of us by the Holy Ghost. The declaration of its reality is the declaration of the reality of the indwelling of the Holy Spirit in the heart, and of the subjection of the activities of the Christian heart and life to the control of this extraneous power. He that is led by the Spirit of God is not led by himself or by any element of his own nature, native or acquired, but is led by the Holy Ghost. He has ceased to be what the Scriptures call a "natural man," and has become what they call a "spiritual man"; that is, to translate these terms accurately, he has ceased to be a self-led man and has become a Spirit-led man—a man led and determined in all his activities by the Holy Ghost. It is this extraneousness of the source of these activities which Paul emphasizes first of all when he declares that the sons of God are led by the Spirit of God.

The second matter which is emphasized by his declaration is the controlling power of the influence exerted on the activities of God's children by the Holy Spirit. One is not led, in the sense of our text, when he is merely directed in the way he should go, guided, as we may say, by one who points out the path and leads only by going before in it; or when he is merely upheld while he himself finds or directs himself to the goal.

The Greek language possesses words which precisely express these ideas, but the apostle passes over these and selects a term which expresses determining control over our actions. Some of these other terms are used elsewhere in the Scriptures to set forth appropriate actions of the Spirit with reference to the people of God. For example, our Lord promised His disciples that when the Spirit of Truth should come, He should guide them into all the truth. Here a term is employed which does not express controlling leading, but what we may perhaps call suggestive leading. It is used frequently in the Greek Old Testament of God's guidance of His people, and once, at least, of the Holy Spirit: "Teach us to do Thy will, for Thou art my God; let Thy good Spirit guide us in the land of uprightness." But the term which Paul employs in our text is a much stronger one than this. It is not the proper word to use of a guide who goes before and shows the way, or even of a commanding general, say, who leads an army. It has stamped upon it rather the conception of the exertion of a power of control over the actions of its subject, which the strength of the led one is insufficient to withstand.

This is the proper word to use, for example, when speaking of leading animals, as when our Lord sent His disciples to find the ass and her colt and commanded them "to loose them and lead them to Him" (Matt. xxi. 2); or as when Isaiah declares in the Scripture which was being read by the Eunuch of Ethiopia whom Philip was sent to meet in the desert, "He was led as a sheep to the slaughter." It is applied to the conveying of sick folk—as men who are not in a condition to control their own movements; as, for example, when the good Samaritan set the wounded traveler on his own beast and led him to an inn and took care of him (Luke x. 34); or when Christ commanded the blind man of Jericho "to be led unto Him" (Luke xviii. 40). It is most commonly used of the enforced movements of prisoners; as when we are told that they led Jesus to Caiaphas to the palace (John xviii. 28); or when we are told that they seized Stephen and led him into the council (Acts vi. 12); or that Paul was provided with letters to Damascus unto the synagogues, "that if he found any that were of the Way, he might lead them bound to Jerusalem" (Acts ix. 2). In a word, though the term may, of course, sometimes be used when the idea of force retires somewhat into the background, and is commonly so used when it is transferred from external compulsion to internal influence—as, for example, when we are told that Barnabas took Paul and led him to the apostles (Acts ix. 2), and that Andrew led Simon unto Jesus (John i. 42)— yet the proper meaning of the word includes the idea of control, and the implication of prevailing determination of action never wholly leaves it.

Its use by Paul on the present occasion must be held, therefore, to emphasize the controlling influence which the Holy Spirit exercises over the activities of the children of God in His leading of them. That extraneous power which has come into our hearts making for righteousness, has not come into them merely to suggest to us what we should do—merely to point out to us from within the way in which we ought to walk—merely to rouse within us and keep before our minds certain considerations and inducements toward righteousness. It has come within us to take the helm and to direct the motion of our frail barks on the troubled sea of life. It has taken hold of us as a man seizes the halter of an ox to lead it in the way which he would have it go; as an attendant conducts the sick in leading him to the physician; as the jailer grasps the prisoner to lead him to trial or to the jail. We were slaves to sin; a new power has entered into us to break that bondage—but not that we should be set, rudderless, adrift on the ocean of life; but that we should be powerfully directed on a better course, leading to a better harbor.

Accordingly Paul, when he declares that we have been emancipated from the law of sin and of death by the advent of the law of the Spirit of life in Christ Jesus into our hearts, does not leave it so, as if emancipation were all. He adds, "Accordingly then, we are bound." Though emancipated, still bound! We are bound; but no longer to the flesh, to live after the flesh, but to the Spirit, to live after the Spirit. He hastens, indeed, to point out that this is no hard bondage, but a happy one; that sons is a name better fitted to express its circumstances than "slaves"—that it includes childship and heirship to God and with Christ. But all this blessed assurance operates to exhibit the happy estate of the service into which we have been brought, rather than to alter the nature of it as service. The essence of the new relation is that it also is one of control, though a control by a beneficent and not a cruel power. We do not at all catch Paul's meaning therefore, unless we perceive the strong emphasis which lies on this fact—that those who are led by the Spirit of God are under the control of the Spirit of God. The extraneous power which has come into us, making for righteousness, comes as a controlling power. The children of God are not the directors of their own activities; there is One that dwells in them who is not merely their guide, but their governor and strong regulator. They go, not where they would, but where He would; they do not what they might wish, but what He determines. This it is to be led by the Spirit of God.

It is to be observed, however, on the other hand, that although Paul uses a term here which emphasizes the controlling influence of the Spirit of God over the activities of God's children, he does not represent the action of the Spirit as a substitute for their activities. If one is not led, in the sense of our text, when he is merely guided, it is equally true that one is not led when he is carried. The animal that is led by the attendant, the blind man that is led to Christ, the prisoner that is led to jail—each is indeed under the control of his leader, who alone determines the goal and the pathway; but each also proceeds on that pathway and to that goal by virtue of his own powers of locomotion.

There was a word lying at the apostle's hand by which he could have expressed the idea that God's children are borne by the Spirit's power to their appointed goal of holiness, apart from any activities of their own, had He elected to do so. It is employed by Peter when he would inform us how God gave His message of old to His prophets. "For no prophecy," he tells us, "ever came by the will of man: but men spake from God, being borne by the Holy Ghost." This term, "borne," emphasizes, as its fundamental thought, the fact that all the power productive of the motion suggested is inherent in, and belongs entirely to, the mover. Had Paul intended to say that God's children are taken up as it were in the Spirit's arms and borne, without effort on their own part, to their destined goal, he would have used this word. That he has passed over it and made use of the word "led" instead, indicates that, in his teaching, the Holy Spirit leads and does not carry God's children to their destined goal of holiness; that while the Spirit determines both the end and the way toward it, His will controlling their action, yet it is by their effort that they advance to the determined end.

Here, therefore, there emerges an interesting indication of the difference between the Spirit's action in dealing with the prophet of God in imparting through him God's message to men, and the action of the same Spirit in dealing with the children of God in bringing them into their proper holiness of life. The prophet is "borne" of the Spirit; the child of God is "led." The prophet's attitude in receiving a revelation from God is passive, purely receptive; he has no part in it, adds nothing to it, is only the organ through which the Spirit delivers it to men; he is taken up by the Spirit, as it were, and borne along by Him by virtue of the power that resides in the Spirit, which is natural to Him, and which, in its exercise, supersedes the natural activities of the man. Such is the import of the term used by Peter to express it. On the other hand, the son of God is not purely passive in the hands of the sanctifying Spirit; he is not borne, but led—that is, his own efforts enter into the progress made under the controlling direction of the Spirit; he supplies, in fact, the force exerted in attaining the progress, while yet the controlling Spirit supplies the entire directing impulse. Such is the import of the term used by Paul to express it. Therefore no prophet could be exhorted to work out his own message with fear and trembling; it is not left to him to work it out—the Holy Spirit works it out for him and communicates it in all its rich completeness to and through him. But the children of God are exhorted to work out their own salvation in fear and trembling because they know the Spirit is working in them both the willing and the doing according to His own good pleasure.

In order to appreciate this element of the apostle's teaching at its full value it is perhaps worth while to observe still further that in his choice of a term to express the nature of the Spirit's action in leading God's children the apostle avoids all terms which would attribute to the Spirit the power employed in making progress along the chosen road. Not only does he not represent us as being carried by the Spirit; he does not even declare that we are drawn by Him. There was a term in common use which the apostle could have used had he intended to express the idea that the Spirit drags, by physical force as it were, the children of God onward in the direction in which He would have them go. This term is actually used when the Saviour declares that no man can come unto Him except the Father draw him (John vi. 44)—which is as much as to say that men in the first instance do not and cannot come to Christ by virtue of any powers native to themselves, but require the action upon them of a power from without, coming to them, drawing their inert, passive weight to Christ, if they are to be brought to Him at all. We can identify this act of drawing—"dragging" would perhaps express the sense of the Greek term none too strongly—with that act which we call, in our theological analysis, regeneration, and which we explain in accordance with the import of this term, as the monergistic act of God, impinging on a sinner who is and remains, as far as this act is concerned, purely passive, and therefore does not move, but is moved.

Such, however, is not the method of the Spirit's leading of which Paul speaks in our text. This is not a drawing or dragging of a passive weight toward a goal which is attained, if attained at all, only by virtue of the power residing in the moving Spirit; but a leading of an active agent to an end determined indeed by the Spirit, and along a course which is marked out by the Spirit, but over which the soul is carried by virtue of its own power of action and through its own strenuous efforts. If we are not borne by the Spirit out of our sin into holiness with a smooth and easy movement, almost unnoted by us or noted only with the languid pleasure with which a child resting peacefully on its mother's breast may note its progress up some rough mountain road, so neither are we dragged by the Spirit as a passive weight over the steep and rugged path. We are led. We are under His control and walk in the path in which He sets our feet. It is His part to keep us in the path and to bring us at length to the goal. But it is we who tread every step of the way; our limbs that grow weary with the labor; our hearts that faint, our courage that fails —our faith that revives our sinking strength, our hope that instills new courage into our souls—as we toil on over the steep ascent.

And thus it is most natural that the third matter to which Paul's declaration that we are led by the Spirit of God directs our attention concerns the pathway over which our progress is made.

One is not led who is unconscious of the road over which he advances; such a one is rather carried. He who is led treads the road himself, is aware of its roughness and its steepness, pants with the effort which he expends, is appalled by the prospect of the difficulties that open out before him, rejoices in the progress made, and is filled with exultant hope as each danger and obstacle is safely surmounted. He who is led is in the hands of an extraneous power, of a power which controls his actions; but the pathway over which he is thus led is trodden by his own efforts —by his own struggles it may be—and the goal that is attained is attained at the cost of his own labor.

When Paul chooses this particular term, therefore, and declares that the sons of God are led by the Spirit, he is in no way forgetful of the arduous nature of the road over which they are to advance, or of the strenuous exertion on their own part by which alone they may accomplish it. He strengthens and comforts them with the assurance that they are not to tread the path alone; but he does not lull them into inertness by suggesting that they are not to tread it. The term he employs avouches to them the constant and continuous presence with them of the leading Spirit, not merely setting them in the right path, but keeping them in it and leading them through it; for it designates not an impulse which merely initiates a movement in a given direction, but a continuous influence unbrokenly determining a movement to its very goal. But his language does not promise them relief from the weariness of the journey, alleviation of the roughness of the road, freedom from difficulty or danger in its course, or emancipation from the labor of travel. That they have been placed in the right path, that they will be kept continuously in it, that they will attain the goal—of this he assures them; for this it is to be led of the Spirit of God, a power not ourselves controlling our actions, prevalently directing our movement to an end of His choice. But He does not encourage us to relax our own endeavors; for he who is led, even though it be by the Spirit of God, advances by virtue of his own powers and his own efforts. In a word, Paul chooses language to express the action of the Spirit on the sons of God which is in perfect harmony with his exhortation to the children of God to which we have already alluded—to work out their own salvation with fear and trembling because they know it is God that is working in them both the willing and the doing according to His own good pleasure.

What a strong consolation for us is found in this gracious assurance—poor, weak children of men as we are! To our frightened ears the text may come at first as with the solemnity of a warning: "As many as are led by the Spirit of God, these and these only are sons of God." Is there not a declaration here that we are not God's children unless we are led by God's Spirit? Knowing ourselves, and contemplating the course of our lives and the character of our ambitions, dare we claim to be led by the Spirit of God? Is this life—this life that I am living in the flesh—is this the product of the Spirit's leading? Shall not despair close in upon me as I pass the dreadful judgment on myself that I am not led by God's Spirit, and that I am, therefore, not one of His sons? Let us hasten to remind ourselves, then, that such is not the purport nor the purpose of the text. It stands here not in order to drive us to despair, because we see we have sin within us; but to kindle within us a great fire of hope and confidence because we perceive we have the Holy Spirit within us.

Paul, as we have seen, does not forget the sin within us. Who has painted it and its baleful power with more vigorous touch? But neither would he have us forget that we have the Holy Spirit within us, and what that blessed fact, above all blessed facts, means. He would not have us reason that because sin is in us we cannot be

God's children; but in happy contradiction to this, that because the Holy Spirit is in us we cannot but be God's children. Sin is great and powerful; it is too great and too powerful for us; but the Holy Ghost is greater and more powerful than even sin. The discovery of sin in us might bring us to despair did not Paul discern the Holy Spirit in us—who is greater than sin—that he may quicken our hope.

This declaration that frightens us is not written, then, to frighten, but to console and to enhearten. It stands here for the express purpose of comforting those who would despair at the sight of their sin. Is there a conflict of sin and holiness in you? asks Paul. This very fact that there is conflict in you is the charter of your salvation. Where the Holy Spirit is not, there conflict is not; sin rules undisputed lord over the life. That there is conflict in you, that you do not rest in complacency in your sin, is a proof that the Spirit of God is within you, leading you to holiness. And all who are led by the Spirit of God are the children of God; and if children, then heirs, heirs of God and joint heirs with Christ Jesus. This is the purport of the message of the text to us. Paul points us not to the victory of good over evil, but to the conflict of good with evil—not to the end but to the process—as the proof of childship to God. The note of the passage is, thus, not one of fear and despair, but one of hope and triumph. "If God be for us who can be against us?"—that is the query the apostle would have ring in our hearts. Sin has a dreadful grasp upon us; we have no power to withstand it. But there enters our hearts a power not ourselves making for righteousness. This power is the Spirit of the most high God. "If God be for us who can be against us?" Let our hearts repeat this cry of victory to-day.

And as we repeat it, let us go onward, in hope and triumph, in our holy efforts. Let our slack knees be strengthened and new vigor enter our every nerve. The victory is assured. The Holy Spirit within us cannot fail us. The way may be rough; the path may climb the dizzy ascent with a rapidity too great for our faltering feet; dangers, pitfalls are on every side. But the Holy Spirit is leading us. Surely, in that assurance, despite dangers and weakness, and panting chest and swimming head, we can find strength to go ever forward.

In these days, when the gloom of doubt if not even the blackness of despair, has settled down on so many souls, there is surely profit and strength in the certainty that there is a portal of such glory before us, and in the assurance that our feet shall press its threshold at the last. In this assurance we shall no longer beat our disheartened way through life in dumb despondency, and find expression for our passionate but hopeless longings only in the wail of the dreary poet of pessimism :—

> "But if from boundless spaces no answering voice shall start,
> Except the barren echo of our ever yearning heart—
> Farewell, then, empty deserts, where beat our aimless wings,
> Farewell, then, dream sublime of uncompassable things."

We are not, indeed, relieved from the necessity for healthful effort, but we can no longer speak of "vain hopes." The way may be hard, but we can no longer talk of "the unfruitful road which bruises our naked feet." Strenuous endeavor may be required of us, but we can no longer feel that we are "beating aimless wings," and can expect no further response from the infinite expanse than "a sterile echo of our own eternal longings." No, no—the language of despair falls at once from off our souls. Henceforth our accents will be borrowed rather from a nobler "poet of faith," and the blessing of Asher will seem to be spoken to us also :—

"Thy shoes shall be iron and brass,
And as thy days, so shall thy strength be.
There is none like unto God, O Jeshurun,
Who rideth upon the heavens for thy help,
And in His excellency on the skies.
The eternal God is thy dwelling-place,
And underneath are the everlasting arms."

VII

PAUL'S EARLIEST GOSPEL

VII

PAUL'S EARLIEST GOSPEL

"We give thanks to God always for you all, . . . knowing, brethren beloved of God, your election. . . . For God appointed us not unto wrath, but unto the obtaining of salvation through our Lord Jesus Christ, who died for us, that . . . we should live together with Him. . . . Faithful is He that calleth you, who will also do it."—1 THES. i. 2, 4; v. 9, 24. (R. V.)

I HAVE put together here passages from the beginning and the end of the First Epistle of Paul to the Thessalonians, because, when taken together, these passages afford a succinct statement of the gospel which Paul preached to the Thessalonians, and on the basis of which that apostolic church was built up. It may be of special interest to note Paul's gospel to the Thessalonians because it gives what we may call his primitive gospel. In observing it we are contemplating the teaching of Paul at the beginning of his career.

This first letter to the Thessalonians is the earliest writing that has come down to us from Paul's pen. Is it perhaps also, we may possibly ask, a little crude and unformed in its presentation of Paul's gospel? A glance at the text is enough to reassure us. The gospel Paul preached to the Thessalonians is the same gospel that he preached to the Romans, and the same gospel that he laid upon the hearts of his helpers, Timothy and Titus, to preach when he should no longer be with them. There is no lack of firmness in the lines of it as they are drawn here; no faltering in the expression of the details. We cannot, then, approach its consideration in a purely historical spirit. The gospel Paul preached in those early days to the Thessalonians is the gospel which he preached ever after and is still preaching to-day to the world. It is the gospel that he commends to us as well as to the Thessalonians, and we may without hesitation take it to ourselves as the very gospel of God.

The external history of the carrying of the gospel to the Thessalonians is soon told. Paul had come among them filled with a very vivid sense of his divine mission, in response to the cry of the Macedonian man to come over and help the Greek peoples. He was, more immediately, fresh from the persecution at Philippi, and was pressed in spirit from his experience there (ii. 2). Waxing bold in God he had proclaimed, perhaps with unusual fervor—certainly not in word only, but also in power and in the Holy Ghost and in much assurance (i. 5)—the pure gospel of God's grace; and had not only adorned the doctrine he preached by a life of self-denial for its sake (ii. 9), but also commended it by a loving eagerness and tender pertinacity in enforcing it on the attention of his hearers. Looking back on it all, he describes his yearning after their souls in the beautiful similes of a nursing mother cherishing her children (ii. 7), and of a watchful father consoling and encouraging and testifying to his sons (ii. 11). The Thessalonians had received this gospel, pressed upon them with such affectionate assiduity, with exceptional readiness and exceptional zeal (i. 6, 9; ii. 15). They had recognized the word of the message as what it really was, not the word of man, but the word of God, and had set themselves to obey its commands. As fruitage of their faith the apostle perceives with joy the Christian graces their lives had from the first exhibited—their work of faith and labor of love and patience of hope (i. 3, 8; iv. 9).

In writing back to them to strengthen them in face of the persecution which had meanwhile fallen upon them, and to exhort them to a continuous advance in their Christian life, Paul naturally makes much of the gospel which had wrought so powerfully among them. He calls it affectionately his gospel (i. 4), and reverentially God's gospel (ii. 2), which was his therefore only because, as God's minister in the gospel of Christ (v. 2), he had been approved to be intrusted with it (ii. 4). It is not to himself—his eloquence, the winningness of his appeal, the force of his argumentation, the clearness of his presentation in preaching it—but to the gospel itself with which he was armed, that he ascribes the revolution that had been wrought in the lives of the Thessalonians. He was God's minister in the gospel of Christ indeed, but the gospel was itself God's own word, and it was it that energized, as the word of God, in them that believed (ii. 13). The whole value of his mission, he gives us to understand over and over again, resided just in the gospel he preached—the glad tidings which he was the instrument in bringing to men.

Now, in the words which we have culled out of this epistle for our text, we have this blessed gospel succinctly summarized. The core of it consisted, it is plain, in one and only one simple proclamation; a proclamation, however, which when duly apprehended is not less tremendous in its import and implications than it is simple in its form

—the proclamation, to wit, of "salvation through our Lord Jesus Christ who died for us that we should live together with Him"; or, as in another passage (i. 10) it is even more concisely summed up, the proclamation of "Jesus our deliverer from the coming wrath." "Jesus our deliverer from the coming wrath!" Let us lay that sentence well to mind, for in that one sentence is contained the whole essence of Paul's gospel to the Thessalonians, and the whole essence of his gospel to us.

The whole essence, we say, though not, of course, the entire structure of it. For, as we have hinted, there are tremendous implications involved in this simple proclamation. And these implications Paul did not leave to the inferences of his disciples to work out, but made them rather the subject of explicit instruction. There is, for example, a whole doctrine of sin implied, and a whole doctrine of redemption, and a whole doctrine of the application of redemption to sinful men, and of the relation of God's activities to the activities of man in the saving process. For, be it observed, to say that the core of Paul's gospel consisted in the simple proclamation of Jesus our deliverer from the coming wrath—of salvation through our Lord Jesus Christ, who died for us that we should live with Him—is not the same as to say that he preached Jesus *simpliciter*. He did not preach Jesus *simpliciter*. He preached, as he elsewhere puts it, Jesus *as crucified* (1 Cor. ii. 2). And the very essence of his proclamation as a gospel consists in just this, that it was not Jesus as man or even as God-man merely that he held up to men's adoring gaze, but Jesus "our deliverer from the coming wrath," Jesus "who died for us that we should live with Him," that he offered to their trusting faith. And this mode of presenting Jesus has, as we say, its tremendous implications—implications of such import that without them the proclamation would be vain, and therefore of such importance as to be made by Paul the subject of explicit and eager teaching.

It will doubtless be of interest, and certainly it is of importance to us in our spiritual apprehension of the truth, to try to draw out somewhat fully the essential characteristics of Paul's gospel as exhibited in this his earliest presentation of it in written form.

The first thing that strongly impresses us, if we scrutinize it closely, is that it is emphatically a gospel of deliverance from sin.

It is a gospel of salvation; and just because it

is a gospel of salvation, behind it there lies the deepest possible sense of sin—active in the apostle's mind as the basis of his whole gospel, and frankly presuppposed as also lying in his readers' minds as a fundamental conviction, the point of entrance, indeed, of his gospel into their hearts. This background of sin is manifested in the words which we have taken as our text, in a double implication. First, there is the contrast drawn in the declaration, " For God appointed us not unto wrath, but unto the obtaining of salvation." Here we see the background of sin as guilt set before us. Those who do not obtain this salvation remain under the wrath of God; and the condition of man wherefrom he requires salvation is therefore a condition of wrath-deserving sin. Again, there is the contrast underlying the declaration, "Faithful is He who calleth you, who will also do it"—for this great assertion is made to comfort those who despair of attaining a blameless life in God's sight. We see here the background of sin as pollution, producing inability to good. It is only in that God who in this crisp proverb is declared not only the caller, but the doer—the one who emphatically performs —that man can trust for the cleansing of his heart. In both aspects of it—guilt and pollution

—sin lies everywhere presupposed as the primary condition of Paul's gospel.

Not least do we perceive its shadow, of course, in that most pregnant of all the declarations of the epistle—that which sums up Paul's gospel in the proclamation of "Jesus our deliverer from the coming wrath." It is clear that before all else this preacher is impressed with the fact that the wrath of God hangs imminent over mankind, and that the great black cloud of sin rests loweringly over the entire world. It is because of this sense of sin that the need of deliverance looms so big in his mind; and that it is such good news, such glad tidings to his heart that Jesus is our deliverer from the coming wrath—that in His death and resurrection we have salvation from the wrath that otherwise would be appointed to us. All Paul's gospel thus rests on sin as its precedent occasion and the measure of its need, and the measure, therefore, of its preciousness.

Now it may well be that this sense of sin that supplied to Paul the dark background against which the glory of the gospel was thrown out, is not so deep or so poignant in our modern world as it was to him or even to his hearers. We hear a good deal, at all events, to-day of the "vanishing sense of sin"; and indeed, when we look around us, we see influences enough at work which must tend to dull men's feeling of the depth and heinousness of sin. Is it, perchance, merely unwitting error into which we fall because of our as yet insufficient knowledge or wisdom? Is it possibly merely the mark of our finiteness, the indication that we are not as yet all that we are hereafter to be? Is it perhaps but the effect of our insufficient adjustment to our environment, that will pass away as we fit ourselves more perfectly into our place? Is it perhaps just the mark of our advancing evolution to the perfection toward which we are constantly progressing —the condition of our advance, because the galling of the imperfections yet remaining and the incitement to effort for their removal? So men to-day talk mildly of what to the apostle was sin in all the hideous suggestions of that word— rotting corruption of heart, throwing itself up in an unclean and polluted life on the one hand; remorseful guilt in the sight of a holy God, entailing His wrath and His wrath's inevitable punishment on the other. And we shall never understand or participate in this gospel which Paul preached to the Thessalonians, and through them to us, until we feel with him the fact and the horror and the helplessness and the hopelessness of the sin that lies as its prime presupposition at its base.

We must note then, secondly, that just because Paul's gospel to the Thessalonians was emphatically a gospel of deliverance from sin, it was as emphatically an ethical gospel—a gospel of righteousness and holiness of life.

In Paul's own summary of it, in the second epistle, this characteristic is thrown forward into very special prominence. The salvation which he makes the substance of his proclamation he there describes as finding its whole sphere just in "sanctification of the Spirit," that is, in the work of the Holy Spirit framing the life into holiness. This note is equally a fundamental note of this first epistle. It is just because of their Christian graces—the revolution thus wrought in their lives —that Paul thanks God in behalf of his converts (i. 3). It is that God may establish their hearts unblamable before our God and Father—that they may be sanctified wholly, and in spirit and in soul and in body be preserved blameless (v. 23)— that he offers his most fervent prayers for them. He declares with strong asseveration that it is the will of God for them that they should abstain from fleshly lusts and be sanctified—for, he explains with insistent iteration, "God called us not for uncleanness but in sanctification" (iv. 8). It is the holy walk alone, he declares, that is pleasing to God (iv. 1); and nothing can exhibit more plainly one's ignorance of God, he intimates, than that he should walk in uncleanness—for, says the apostle, God is our judge in all these things, and of this he had faithfully forewarned his readers and testified (iv. 6, 7). Thus the very essence of their calling is made to consist in holiness of life, and Paul obviously looks upon their holiness as the direct result of their salvation, or, let us say rather, as the very matter of their salvation. Their salvation consists just in holiness, and in so far as it exists at all it is manifested in the sanctification in which it consists.

So far, then, is Paul from lending any countenance to that odd fancy which has shown itself here and there through all the ages—that would look upon religion and morality in divorce, and esteem the one possible in the absence of the other—that he absolutely identifies the two in his gospel. This, of course, implies that with him religion is something more than a mere sentiment of awe in the presence of a superhuman power; and morality something more than mere external conformity to a standard of human custom or to laws of life of human exactment. To understand his standpoint we must apprehend all that is meant by religion conceived as communion with the holy God in Christ Jesus the righteous one, and by morality conceived as Godlikeness, as conformity to the likeness of God's own Son. He was not proclaiming an abstract "religion"; he was proclaiming the concrete religion of salvation from the wrath of God through Jesus Christ, and as this salvation is from sin it necessarily is unto holiness—that holiness without which no one shall see God. But we must not, on the other hand, suppose that Paul conceived this salvation and holiness as working its whole process all at once; or looked upon his converts, if believers at all, as wholly free from sin. Nothing is clearer than his solicitude for them as *viatores* who have not yet attained the goal; nothing is more striking than his tenderness with them in their remaining sin, and the zeal of his exhortations to them to go on to perfection.

We have not reached the bottom of the matter, therefore, until we observe, again, that Paul's gospel of salvation from sin, which he preached to the Thessalonians, was emphatically an eschatological gospel.

As we have seen, Paul was under no illusions, nor did he permit his readers to remain under any illusions, as to the nature of the life they had been leading in the world, or as to the need that they had of "salvation" with reference to this their life in this world—if they would at all be well-pleasing to God. The change that had come over them, the new life that had become theirs when "they turned unto God from idols to serve the living and true God"—their "work of faith and labor of love and patience of hope"—formed the very matter of his thanksgiving to God in their behalf. And one of the chief objects of his writing to them now was strenuously to urge them to increase and abound in love to one another (iii. 11), to abound more and more in the holy walk which alone is pleasing to God (iv. 7); and to press on their consciences the fact that the will of God toward them was their sanctification and His call to them was unto sanctification (iv. 3, 7); and at the same time to comfort them, in their sense of hopeless shortcoming, with the assurance of the faithfulness and ability of the God who had called them to complete the good work unto the end (iv. 23).

Nevertheless this strong insistence upon the salvation of their earthly life to holiness by no means exhausted his saving message; nor did it constitute its primary element. His eye is set steadily not upon the present, but upon the future. Even this holiness of life on which he lays such stress is, indeed, not looked upon as primarily for this life, but rather as having its chief significance for the life to come. This is distinctly its reference, for example, in Paul's fervent prayers for their perfecting in holiness and in his comforting promises concerning it. We read, "The Lord make you to increase and abound in love toward one another, and toward all men, . . . to the end He may stablish your hearts unblamable in holiness before our God and Father, at the coming of our Lord Jesus with all His saints" (iii. 12, 13). We read, "And the God of peace Himself sanctify you wholly; and may your spirit and soul and body be preserved entire, without blame, at the coming of our Lord Jesus Christ; faithful is He that calleth you, who will also do it" (vs. 23, 24). Thus their very sanctification, on which he lays such stress and in which he makes the very matter of their "salvation" to consist, is yet looked upon by him not in and for itself, but as a means to an end—as a preparation for something to come—in which something to come their real salvation finds its culmination and its crown.

It is emphatically, therefore, an eschatological salvation that Paul preached to the Thessalonians. And accordingly this epistle that he writes to them is a markedly eschatological epistle. His mind was set upon the future, and he kept his readers' minds also set upon the future. The salvation he was proclaiming to them was a matter not of present fruition, but distinctly of hope. To arm themselves for the temptations of life they are to put on the breastplate of faith and love, and for a helmet the hope of salvation (iii. 8). What he desires in them, then, is an attitude not of attainment, but of expectation. When they turned unto God from idols it was to serve the living and the true God, and to wait for His Son from heaven (i. 10). Whatever comes to them here and now, therefore, in the way of enjoyment of this salvation is prelibation only. The realization belongs not here, but yonder; not now, but in the time to come.

The hinge of the whole proclamation turns, in a word, on a doctrine of wrath to come, which impends over all, deliverance from which can be had only in Jesus Christ—in His death in our behalf and His resurrection as the firstfruits of those that sleep. Accordingly the very core of Paul's gospel to the Thessalonians is summed up, as we have seen, in the proclamation of Jesus our deliverer from the wrath to come. And when the apostle would encourage his readers in the prospect of that dread coming of the Lord as a thief in the night, bringing sudden destruction, as travail upon a woman with child, on all who have not obeyed His gospel, it is in the carefully chosen words, "For God appointed us not unto wrath, but unto the obtaining of salvation through our Lord Jesus Christ, who died for us that we should live with Him." The salvation they hoped for is thus set pointedly over against the wrath appointed for mankind outside its reach; and it is set forth most sharply as distinctly an eschatological salvation.

Accordingly, also, nothing that in this world befalls those who are appointed to the obtaining of this salvation can mar their joy in believing. Not a life of suffering and persecution. Indeed, to that too they are appointed (ii. 3). And whatever may be the distress and the affliction that assault them here, there remains a far more exceeding weight of glory in store for them hereafter. And not death itself. For death itself is but a sleep for those who believe that Christ died and rose again, and that God will bring them with Him. And when He shall descend from heaven with a shout, with the voice of the archangel and with the trump of God, they shall rise from the dead to be henceforth for ever with the Lord.

This is a gospel, obviously, then, not of temporal salvation from present-day evils, but of eternal salvation from the endless burnings of the wrath of God against sin; not of temporal salvation to present-day excellences, but of eternal salvation to everlasting glory. We have heard a good deal of late of very different import. We have been repeatedly told that our concern is not to be with heaven, but with earth; that we should not talk of saving our souls, but rather, simply, of saving our lives; that to get the life right is the main thing, and conduct should be the one end of our endeavor. Let us, it is said, take pains with our adjustments here and see to it that our lives are clean and our activities determined by altruistic motives; and what then remains of duty to man or of hopes or fears with which he need concern himself? Such a gospel is plainly out of all relation with Paul's gospel. So far from beginning and ending with this life, Paul treats this life as but the "suburb of the life elysian, whose portal we call death." To him the real life is there; we are here but pilgrims with no abiding city, and should live as becomes those whose citizenship is elsewhere—in the city that has foundations, whose builder and maker is God. To him all that enters into this life is but a preparation for the life to come, and should be consciously looked upon as such and dealt with as such; certainly not as unimportant, but as finding its importance not in itself, but in its relations to the eternity of bliss or woe, in comparison with which this little stretch of time in which the drama of the earthly life is played out is as nothing.

We cannot feel surprise, then, when we observe, once more, that Paul's gospel to the Thessalonians is distinctly a heterosoteric gospel—that is to say, a gospel that offers us salvation in and by the work of another; and does not simply propose for us a way in which we may save ourselves.

Had he in mind merely some amelioration of the conditions of life in this world—some better adjustment of society and of the individual life with respect to the several duties that press on it in its surroundings—it might have been more possible for him to look to man himself, in his native powers of conscience and sensibility and will, to work the necessary change; though for Paul, with his deep view of sin and of the paralysis that sin induces in all activities toward God, even this would have been really impossible. But when our eye is set not merely upon the adjustments of this life, but upon salvation from the dreadful wrath of God that burns against our sin conceived as guilt, what hope can be placed in man himself, or any power he may be thought to possess, to work out deliverance? Accordingly, Paul preaches a gospel not fundamentally of effort from within, but of deliverance from without. Its core, its substance, as we have repeatedly pointed out, lies in the great proclamation of "Jesus our deliverer from the coming wrath," or, more fully stated, in the offer of "salvation through our Lord Jesus Christ, who died for us that we should live with Him."

It is not merely a salvation, then, that Paul preaches, but above everything else, a Saviour; and the whole nerve of his gospel lies in the assumption that salvation to us men, immersed in sin and cowering under the righteous wrath of God, were impossible save through this Saviour. Therein, indeed, lies its whole character as a gospel, good news, glad tidings. To us, helpless and hopeless in our sins, unable to free ourselves from either the tyranny or curse of sin, Paul comes proclaiming a deliverer, in whose hands lies salvation. For, as we have already said, it is not Jesus *simpliciter* that constitutes the substance of Paul's gospel, but, as he phrases it elsewhere, Jesus *as crucified* (1 Cor. ii. 2)—Jesus our deliverer from the coming wrath—salvation through Jesus Christ, who died for us that we should live together with Him.

It does not fall in Paul's way in this brief epistle to give any very full description of how Jesus saves from wrath. But enough is dropped incidentally to assure us of the outlines of His doctrine even here. Clearly the stress is thrown not on our Lord's person, but on His work. Not, of course, as if His person were treated as of no importance. He is ever "the Lord" to Paul (i. 6; ii. 15; iv. 1, 2, 15, 16, 17; v. 2, 12, 28), and that in the most exalted sense; or, with loving appropriation, "our Lord" (i. 2; iii. 11, 13; v. 9, 24, 28). He is God's unique Son (i. 10), in whom all Christian graces move as their sphere (i. 3; iii. 8; iv. 1, 2), and who along with God is the determiner of the ways of men (iii. 11), and from whom grace is invoked for men (iii. 13; v. 28). But the entire stress of the proclamation is thrown on His having become our deliverer from the coming wrath specifically through His work on our behalf—and more particularly by His death for us (v. 10).

With His death the resurrection of Christ is connected as the object of faith for believers (i. 10; iv. 14); and with these His second coming from heaven, to close the drama on earth with a final assize, is associated as the object of the Christian's loving expectation (i. 10; ii. 19; iii. 13; iv. 14, 15, 17; v. 2, 23), since in it his salvation will be completed. But it is especially the death of Christ that is signalized as the hinge of His saving grace. He died for us that we should live with Him (v. 10). It is that He died and rose again that we must believe (iv. 14) if we are to be brought with Him at the last day. It was, in a word, in His death that He, whom God has raised from the dead and who now sits in heaven waiting until the time of His return shall arrive—the day of the Lord, which shall come not when men expect it, but when it suits His ends—has accomplished our salvation, our deliverance from the wrath to come.

And it is precisely at this point that we reach the center of the center, the heart of the heart of Paul's gospel. The glad tidings he bore to the Thessalonians were tidings of death—of a hideous death, a death which he can think of only with horror and with reprobation of those who inflicted it. "Who hath killed the Lord," he says—instinctively arranging the words so as to bring out the enormity of the deed: "who it was who the very Lord Himself have killed, Jesus, and also the prophets"—when his indignation arises against the Jews who are piling up their sins always, and over whom the wrath of God is, he says, hanging like a surcharged cloud ready to burst. But it was a death, on the other hand, that in another aspect of it was a glorious death— a death for us by which we are saved from death, and Christ is made our deliverer. "He died for us that we should live with Him!" There is the very kernel of Paul's gospel.

It will scarcely require emphasizing, therefore, that Paul's gospel to the Thessalonians was, further, emphatically a supernaturalistic gospel.

A gospel that comes proclaiming salvation to sinful men by the death of the Son of God—slain, indeed, by the wicked hands of men to their own undoing, but slain, on the other hand, in His own purpose, for the deliverance of His people from the coming wrath—must needs be supernaturalistic to the core. And so it is in every item of Paul's representation of it. The deliverance which it proclaims is a deliverance more especially, not from earthly ills or even from earthly suffering, but from the wrath to come.

And as Paul tears aside the veil that hides the future, he tears aside with it the veil that covers the vast reaches of the heavenly places, and bids us raise our eyes from the earth and the forces that operate in the ordinary events of the earth, and look up to that broader stage where the drama of eternity is being played. The very eschatological character of the deliverance which he is announcing involves an emphasis on the supernatural which is almost extreme. Hence we are bidden to seek not on earth but in heaven for our deliverer (i. 10); whence also He is to come in His own time—with all His saints—and those that have fallen asleep in Jesus are to rise, to be caught up on the clouds and to meet Him in the air as He descends from heaven with a shout, with the voice of the archangel and with the trump of God. There is surely no chariness of the supernatural in the painting of this scene; and this is the scene of the final act in the drama of salvation.

But no less really supernaturalistic is Paul's conception of those processes in the working out of the deliverance which appeal less to the outward eye as the wonderful works of God; but to his inner apprehension clearly evinced themselves as nevertheless equally of God. How is this tremendous deliverance, for example, made the possession of men? How was it that he himself and these Thessalonian Christians to whom he was writing were made sharers in this great deliverance? To Paul this too was directly of God. He conceived it, in his gospel, as just as supernatural an occurrence as the blast of the trumpet of God itself, at that day, which shall raise the dead. This is, indeed, suggested to us in the words we have taken as our text; or, to speak more correctly, it is the open assertion of every one of the clauses which we have brought together in the text. It is, for example, to God that he gives thanks for the Christian virtues of his converts. Why? He tells us himself. It is because the very fact that they are Christians at all, that they received the gospel he brought to them, as well as all the subsequent fruits of their new lives, are proof of their election thereunto. Wherefrom it is easy to infer that in his view it is of God alone that man believes in the gospel of deliverance through His dear Son. Again, when he would prepare his readers for the prospect of the sudden coming of Christ as avenger upon those who are not in Him, he does it, not by pointing to anything that they can do for themselves to escape the impending doom, but by assuring them that they have been appointed of God not to wrath, but to the obtaining of salvation. And, once again, when he would encourage them, in their known shortcomings, yet to hope for a blameless standing before the judgment seat of God, he does it, not by appealing to their own powers of will and action, and so stirring them up to new endeavors, but by pointing to God: "Faithful is He that calleth you, who also will do it." In each and every case, in fine, it is to God that he raises their eyes as to the author of all that is good within them, as well as of all that is good in store for them. That they are in Christ at all is of God; that they shall abide in Him is of God; that they shall be fit to receive the reward in the end is of God. It is all of God and nothing at all of it is of themselves. From this plane of high supernaturalism in the application of the salvation wrought by the death of Christ the apostle departs in no single word in the whole epistle.

Participation in this salvation is certainly suspended on the proclamation and acceptance of the gospel. The very ground of Paul's thanks to God in behalf of the Thessalonians is that they had accepted the gospel (i. 2, 6; ii. 13). The very ground of his joy in being approved of God to be intrusted with this gospel turns on the inestimable importance of its proclamation; and Paul spared himself in nothing that he might proclaim it and proclaim it in its purity and with eager zeal (ii. 1). He distinctly declares, indeed, that the salvation of men depends on the gospel reaching them, and makes it accordingly one of the chief counts in his terrible arraignment of the Jews that they showed themselves haters of men in forbidding him to speak to the Gentiles that they might be saved (ii. 16). Obviously, where the gospel is not conveyed, there is no salvation; where the gospel, though conveyed, is not accepted, there is no salvation.

But it does not at all follow, and Paul does not permit his readers for a moment to imagine that in his view it followed, that nothing is implied in its acceptance beyond opportunity to hear the gospel and a native movement of the natural will toward its acceptance. To him, on the contrary, man as a sinner is not an accepter of the gospel proclamation. That he ever accepts it is due proximately to a "call" from God—a call that operates within, at the center of his activities; and ultimately to his selection by God to be a recipient of His grace. Accordingly, it is God that Paul thanks for the entrance of his readers into the Christian life and hope, and it is to His election that he traces the fact of their acceptance of the gospel (ii. 2). And he emphatically declares that it is God that called His converts into His own kingdom and glory (ii. 13)—into His *own* kingdom and glory, as one would say, Who else can have the power to dispose of these but He? (iv. 7). Accordingly, too, Paul points his readers to this God who has called us not for uncleanness, but in sanctification, as to one who employs a mode of action which will not let his purpose in the call fail: "Faithful is He that calleth you, who also will do it." This "caller," in other words, is emphatically also the "performer."

So little does there lie in Paul's mind a sense of inconsistency between the two ideas of salvation coming to men through their acceptance of the truth and salvation communicated to men by the appointment of God, that in the central passage of all, in which the terms of his gospel are most fully set forth, he brings the two ideas together in the most significant manner. Fear not, he says, for God appointed us, "not unto wrath, but "—you will observe he does not say simply "but unto salvation," but, bringing out our personal act in receiving it, "but unto the obtaining, the acquisition of salvation through

our Lord Jesus Christ." It is our "acquisition"
—this salvation; and it comes to none who do
not receive it. But that we acquire it, that we
receive it by whatever subjective act, is only because of our appointment thereunto by God; or,
as Paul puts it in the parallel passage in the
second epistle, because "God has chosen us from
the beginning unto salvation in sanctification of
the Spirit and belief of the truth, whereunto He
called us through the gospel unto the obtaining
of the glory of our Lord Jesus Christ" (2 Thes.
ii. 13).

Thus, whenever Paul touches on the matter,
he takes us at once back to God, and exhibits in
the fullest light the inherent supernaturalism of
His gospel. It is a gospel of salvation by the
mighty power of God, prepared for in our eternal
election, applied in our effectual call, completed
by a prevalent keeping, and issuing at last in
entrance into glory—all through the constant
work of God, the faithful performer.

It is plain, therefore, that Paul's gospel to the
Thessalonians was a gospel in which all the glory
is given to God.

Its note from beginning to end is the note of
soli Deo gloria. It is God, we repeat, whom he

thanks for every Christian grace that he discovers in his readers. It is to God that he ascribes their very acceptance of the gospel that was offered them—to God who "called" them into His own kingdom and glory. It is to God that he ascribes every step they take in the life of holiness into which they have been called. It is to God that he prays that they may be perfected in their sanctification, and presented blameless before the throne of judgment at the last day. It is to God that he ascribes their keeping until that dread event. It is on God's faithfulness—the faithfulness of Him that calls—that he hangs all his and his converts' hopes of escaping the wrath they know they deserve: "Faithful is He that calleth you, who also will do it."

It is all of God; nothing is, in the ultimate analysis, of man. Man provides only the sinner to be saved: God provides the entire salvation. And though it is a man that God saves, and though He saves him, therefore, as a man, and as a man in the full exercise of all his activities that belong to him as a man—so that he is saved by the acceptance of the truth, in a life of holiness, through a perseverance in sanctification to the end—yet it is always and ever God to whom the acceptance, the walk, the endurance is due; who, in a word, is working at every step and in every stage both the willing and the doing in accordance with His own good pleasure. The details of God's modes of operation in bringing the vessels of His election, whom He has appointed not to wrath but to the obtaining of salvation, to entrance into His own kingdom and glory, are indeed little dwelt upon here. We hear of the Holy Spirit as the agent in performing the work, certainly (iv. 8; i. 5, 6; [v. 19]), but only incidentally, without pause for explanation. But the fact of the dependence of the whole process of salvation on the loving will of the Father, who selects and calls and sanctifies and glorifies whom He will, is the underlying assumption in every allusion. The *soli Deo gloria* sounds from end to end of the epistle as its dominant note.

And therefore, finally, the gospel of Paul to the Thessalonians is emphatically a gospel of faith, a gospel of trust.

The terms "believe" and "faith" do not occur with any especial frequency in this epistle (i. 7; ii. 10, 13; iv. 4; i. 3, 8; iii. 2, 5; vi. 10; v. 8). But the thing is a fundamental note of the whole letter. Just because the whole of salvation as proclaimed in Paul's gospel, in each of its steps and stages, runs back to God as its author and furtherer, a continual sense of humble dependence on God and of loving trust in Him is by it formed and fostered in every heart into which it makes entrance. Under the teachings of this gospel the eye is withdrawn from self and the face turned upward in loving gratitude to God, the great giver.

Now this attitude of trust and dependence on God is just the very essence of religion. In proportion as any sense of self-sufficiency or any dependence on self enters the heart, in that proportion religion is driven from it. And what other attitude is becoming or, indeed, possible in weak and sinful man? Can he wrest salvation from the unwilling hands of God? Can he retain it in his powerless grasp when once it is given him? No. If he is to be saved at all, it must be God that saves him; and the beginning and middle and end of his salvation must be alike of God. Every sinner, when once aroused to the sense of his sin, knows this for himself—knows it in the times of his clearest vision and deepest comprehension with a poignancy that drives him to despair. Paul's gospel meets the sinner's need; it provides a salvation from without, every step of which is of God. And it meets also the highest aspirations of the saint as well: for it justifies and strengthens his instinctive attitude of trust and his ineradicable conviction of dependence on the God of all grace. In one word, Paul's gospel to the Thessalonians, being through and through a gospel of trust, reveals itself to us as a gospel, as the only gospel, in which religion comes to its rights and by which the heart is drawn upward to the great heart of God, and is immovably attached to it in adoring love.

Oh, brethren, was this gospel for the Thessalonians only? Or shall we not hearken to it as also a gospel for us, to-day? Are we not, in our native condition, in like case with those to whom Paul first taught it? We look within us, and what do we see there but foul corruption, festering to spiritual death? We raise our eyes to heaven, and what do we observe there but the wrath of God turned against every doer of iniquity? We cast our eyes forward and peer into the future, and what can we discern as the closing scene of this drama of time in which our parts are cast but a dread day of judgment, when we shall receive the due reward of our wicked hearts and evil deeds? Does not the cry rise to the lips of each of us as that scene takes form more and more sharply in our vision,—

> "That fearful day, that day of speechless dread,
> When Thou shalt come, to judge the quick and dead—
> I shudder to foresee,
> Oh, God, what then shall be?"

Oh, what glad tidings it is to hear of "Jesus our deliverer from the coming wrath"—of a salvation through our Lord Jesus Christ, who has died for us that we should live with Him, to which, rather than to this impending wrath, God has appointed us!

God has appointed us! Let us note that clause —for, ah, do we not know that it is not to this that we have appointed ourselves? Does not the proof of this lie all around us? Did we turn ourselves from our sins, or did we not rather delight ourselves in them? Was it we who sought out the ways of peace and joy, or did we not from the beginning scorn them and love rather the pursuit of evil? Can we even to-day keep our feet from falling? Oh, how we slip! Nay, how we willfully turn aside to do our own deeds! When we observe our ways, do we not know that it is not in us to attain the good? Let us hear, then, the rest of this gospel: "Faithful is

He that calleth you, and it is He who will also do it." As it is He that has given His Son to die for us; as it is He who has appointed us to salvation in Him; as it is He that has called us into communion with His holy life; so it is He who will complete the work He has begun in us—it is He that will bring us in gladness to the goal. Let us trust, then, in Him! Let us trust, then, in Him! For it is in this trust—this trust in God, who is at once our Saviour and our salvation—that begins and centers and ends all our personal religion; that begins and centers and ends all our rational hope; that begins and centers and ends all our salvation. It is He that saves us and not we ourselves. Let us trust, then, in Him! Let us trust in Him!

VIII

FALSE RELIGIONS AND THE TRUE

VIII

FALSE RELIGIONS AND THE TRUE

"What therefore ye worship in ignorance, this set I forth unto you."—ACTS xvii. 23. (R. V.)

THESE words give the gist of Paul's justly famous address at Athens before the court of the Areopagus. The substance of that address was, to be sure, just what the substance of all his primary proclamations to Gentile hearers was, namely, God and the judgment. The necessities of the case compelled him to approach the heathen along the avenue of an awakened conscience. They had not been prepared for the preaching of Jesus by a training under the old covenant, and no appeals to prophecy and its fulfillment could be made to them. God and the judgment necessarily constituted, therefore, the staple of his proclamation to them; and so typical an instance as this address to the Areopagus could not fail to exhibit the characteristics of its class with especial purity.

Nevertheless, the peculiar circumstances in

which it was delivered have imprinted on this address also a particular character of its own. Paul spoke it under a specially poignant sense of the depths of heathen ignorance and of the greatness of heathen need. The whole address palpitates with his profound feeling of the darkness in which the heathen world is immersed, and his eager longing to communicate to it the light intrusted to his care. All that goes before the words selected for the text and all that comes after serve but to enhance their great declaration —build for it, as it were, but a lofty platform upon which it is raised to fix the gaze of men. Out of it all Paul fairly shouts this one essential message to the whole unbelieving world: "What therefore ye worship in ignorance, this set I forth unto you."

Let us consider for a little while the circumstances in which the address was delivered. Summoned by a supernatural vision, Paul had crossed the sea and brought the gospel into Europe. Landing in Macedonia, he had preached in its chief cities, meeting on the one hand with great acceptance, and arousing on the other the intensest opposition. He had been driven from city to city until the brethren had at last fled with him to the sea and, hurrying him upon a ship, had conveyed him far to the south and, at last, landed him at Athens. There they left him—alone but in safety—and returned to Macedonia to send his companions to him.

Meanwhile Paul awaited their coming at Athens. Athens! mother of wisdom, mistress of art; but famous, perhaps, above all its wisdom and above all its art for the intensity of its devotion to the gods. Paul had had a missionary's experience with idolatry, in its grosser and more refined forms alike; he had been forced into contact with it throughout his Asian work. Even so, Athens seems to have been a revelation to him—a revelation which brought him nothing less than a shock. Here he was literally in the thick of it. No other nation was so given over to idolatry as the Athenians. One writer tells us that it was easier to find a god in populous Athens than a man; another, scarcely exaggerating, declares that the whole city was one great altar, one great sacrifice, one great votive offering. The place seemed to Paul studded with idols, and the sight of it all brought him a paroxysm of grief and concern.

He was in Athens, as it were, in hiding. But he could not keep silence. He went to the synagogue on the Sabbath and there preached to the Jews and those devout inquirers who were accustomed to visit the synagogues of the Jews in every city. But this did not satisfy his aroused zeal. He went also to the market place—that agora which the public teachers of the city had been wont to frequent for the propagation of their views—and there, like them, every day, he argued with all whom he chanced to meet. Among these he very naturally encountered certain adherents of the types of philosophy then dominant—the Epicurean and Stoic—and in conflict with them he began to attract attention.

He was preaching, as was his wont, "Jesus" and the "resurrection"—doubtless much as he preached them in his recorded address, to which all this led up. Some turned with light contempt away from him and called him a mere smatterer; others, with perhaps no less contempt, nevertheless took him more seriously and anxiously asked if he were not "a proclaimer of alien divinities." This was an offense in Athens; and so they brought him to the Areopagus. He was not formally arraigned for trial—there was only set on foot something like a preliminary official inquiry; and the question put to him is oddly compounded of courteous suggestion and authoritative demand. They said: "May we be allowed to know what this new teaching is that is talked of by thee? For thou dost bring certain strange things to our ears; and it is our wish to know what these things may be." The hand is gloved, but you see the iron showing through. It was to Paul, however, only another opportunity; and in the conscious authority of his great mission he stood forth in the midst of the court and began to speak.

We must bear in mind that Paul was put to the question on the general charge that he was "a proclaimer of strange deities." He had no intention whatever of denying this general allegation. He was rather firmly determined to seize this opportunity yet once more to proclaim a Deity evidently unknown to the Athenians. And this, in fact, he proceeded at once to do. But he did it after a fashion which disarmed the complaint; which enlisted the Athenians themselves as unwilling indeed, but nevertheless real, worshipers of the God he proclaimed; and which powerfully pried at their consciences as well as appealed to their intelligences and even their national pride to give wings to his proclamation.

The hinge on which the whole speech turns

is obviously Paul's deep sense of the darkness of heathen ignorance. As our Saviour said to the Samaritan woman, so Paul, in effect, says to the Athenian jurists and philosophers, "You worship you know not what." The altar at Athens which he signalizes as especially significant of heathen worship is precisely the altar inscribed "To a Not-known God." The whole course of their heathen development he characterizes as a seeking of God, if by any chance—"in the possible hope at least that"—they may touch Him as a blind man touches with his hands fumblingly what he cannot see—and so doubtfully find Him; nay, shortly and crisply, as "times of ignorance." The very purpose of his proclamation of his gospel among them is to bring light into this darkness, to make them to know the true nature and the real modes of working, the all-inclusive plan and the decisive purpose of the one true God. Therefore it is simply true to say that the hinge on which the whole speech turns is the declaration that the heathen are steeped in ignorance and require, above all things, the light of divine instruction.

But when we have said this we have not said all. After all, it is not quite a blank ignorance that Paul ascribes to the Athenians. He institutes a certain connection between what they worship and the God he was commending to them. He does not wholly scoff at their religion, though he certainly sharply reprobates and deeply despises the modes in which it expresses itself. He does not entirely condemn their worship even of a not-known god; he rather makes it a point of attachment for proclaiming the higher worship of the known God of heaven and earth which he is recommending to them. There is, in a word, a certain amount of recognition accorded by him to their religious feelings and aspirations.

It is accordingly not all a scoff when he tells them that he perceives that they are apparently "very religious." The word he employs is no doubt sometimes used in a bad sense, and accordingly is frequently translated here by the ill-savored word "superstitious." So our English version translates it: "I perceive that in all things ye are too superstitious" or "somewhat superstitious," as the Revised Version puts it. But it is scarcely possible to believe that Paul uses it in this evil sense here. It means in itself nothing but "divinity-fearing"—not exactly "God-fearing," though generally equivalent to that, because it has a hint in it of the gods many and lords many of the heathen. It easily, therefore, lends itself to a bad sense, and is often, as we have seen, so used. But as often it is used in a perfectly good sense, as equivalent simply to "religious," and surely it is so used here. Paul is not charging his hearers with superstition; he is recognizing in them a religious disposition. He chooses a term, indeed, of somewhat non-committal character—which would not say too much—which might be taken perhaps as bearing a subtle implication of incomplete approval: but a word by which he expresses at least no active disapproval and even a certain measure of active approval. Paul, in fine, commends the religiousness of the Athenians.

The forms in which this religiousness expressed itself he does not commend. The sight of them, indeed, threw him into a paroxysm of distress, if not of indignation. He could not view without disgust and horror the degradation of their worship. In one sense we may say that it reached its lowest level in this altar, "To a Not-known God." For what could be worse than the superstitious dread which, after cramming every corner of the city with altars to every conceivable divinity, was not yet satisfied, but must needs feel blindly out after still some other power of earth or air or sky to which to immolate victims or before which to cringe in unintelligent fear? But in another aspect it may even have seemed to Paul that in this altar might rather be seen the least degraded expression of the religious aspirations of the Athenians. Where every definite trait given to their conceptions of divinity was but a new degradation of the idea of the divine, there is a certain advantage attaching to vagueness. At least no distinctive foulness was attributed to a god confessedly unknown. Perhaps just because of its undifferentiation and indefiniteness it might therefore seem a purer symbol of that seeking after God for which God had destined all nations when He appointed to them the ordained times and limits of their habitation, if by any chance they might feel Him and so find Him. Surely the forms they gave to the gods they more definitely conceived, the characters they ascribed to them, the functions they assigned them, and the legendary stories of their activities which they wove around them, sufficiently evinced that in them the Athenians had not so much as fumblingly touched God, much less found Him. A worship offered to "an unknown god" was at least free from the horror of definitely conceiving God as corruptible men and birds and fourfooted beasts and creeping things.

In any event, behind the worship, however ill conceived, Paul sees and recognizes the working of that which he does not shame to call religion. Enshrined within his general condemnation of the heathenism of the Athenians there lies thus a recognition of something not to be condemned—something worthy of commendation rather—fit even on his lips to bear the name of "religion." All this is implied in the words we have chosen as our text, and it is therefore that we have said of them that they give us the gist of the whole address. "What ye thus not knowing adore," says Paul, "that it is that I am proclaiming to you." It will repay us, probably, to probe the matter a little in the way of its wider applications.

First, then, we say there is given in the apostolic teaching a certain recognition to the religion of the heathen.

We do not say, mark you, that a recognition is given to the heathen religions. That is something very different. The heathen religions are uniformly treated as degrading to man and insulting to God. The language of a recent writer which declares that man's "most unfortunate things" are his religions—nay, that man's religions are "among his worst crimes"—is thoroughly justified by the apostolic attitude toward them. Read but the account given at the end of the first chapter of Romans of the origin of these religions in the progressive degradation of man's thought of God, as man's repeated withdrawals from God and God's repeated judicial blindings of man interwork to the steady destruction of all religious insight and all moral perception alike, and from this observe how the writers of the New Testament conceived of the religions which men have in the procession of the ages formed for themselves.

Nor is it to be imagined that only the more degraded of the popular superstitions were in the apostle's mind when he painted this dreadful picture of the fruits of human religious thinking. In an almost contemporary epistle he calmly passes his similar judgment on all the philosophies of the world. Not by all its wisdom, he tells us, has the world come to know God, but in these higher elaborations also, becoming vain in its imaginations, its foolish heart has only become darkened. In a somewhat later epistle he sums up his terrible estimate of the religious condition of the Gentiles in that dreadful declaration that "they walk in the vanity of their mind, being darkened in their understanding, alienated from the life of God, because of the ignorance that is in them, because of the hardening of their heart."

This is what the apostle thought—not of some heathen, but of heathen as such, in their religious life—not of the degraded bushmen of Australia or Africa or New Guinea, but of the philosophic minds of Greece and Rome in the palmiest days of their intellectual development and ethical and æsthetic culture; of the Socrateses and Platos and Aristotles and Epictetuses and Marcus Aureliuses of that ancient world, which some would have us look upon as so fully to have found God as veritably to have taken heaven by storm and to have entered it by force of its own attainments. To him it was, on the contrary, in his briefest phrase, "without hope and without God."

Nevertheless, alongside of and in the very midst of this sweeping and unmitigated condemnation of the total religious manifestation of heathendom there exists an equally constant and distinct recognition of the reality and value of religion even among the heathen. It does not seem ever to have occurred to the writers of the New Testament to doubt that religion is as universal as intelligence itself; or to question the reality or value of this universal religiousness. To them man, as such, appears to be esteemed no more a reasonable creature than a religious animal; and they appeal to his religious instinct and build upon it expectations of a response to their appeal, with the same confidence which they show when they make their appeal to his logical faculty. They apparently no more expect to find a man without religion than they expect to find a man without understanding, and they seem to attach the same fundamental value to his inherent religiousness as to his inherent rationality.

In this the passage that is more particularly before us to-day is thoroughly representative of the whole New Testament. Paul, it is seen at once, does not here in any way question the fact that the Athenians are religious, any more than he questions that they are human beings. He notes, rather, with satisfaction that they are very especially religious. "I perceive that ye are in all things exceedingly divinity-fearing." There is a note of commendation in that which is unmistakable. Nor does he betray any impulse to denounce their religious sentiment as intrinsically evil. On the contrary, he takes it frankly as the basis of his appeal to them. In effect, he essays merely to direct and guide its functioning, and in so doing recognizes it as the foundation of all the religious life which he would, as the teacher of Christianity to them, fain see developed in and by them. In the same spirit he always deals with what we may call the inherent religiousness of humanity. Man, as such, in his view is truly and fundamentally religious.

Now this frank recognition, or, we might better say, this emphatic assertion of the inherent religiousness of humanity, constitutes a fact of the first importance in the biblical revelation. It puts the seal of divine revelation on the great fundamental doctrine that there exists in man a *notitia Dei insita*—a natural knowledge of God, which man can no more escape than he can escape from his own humanity. Endowed with an ineradicable sense of dependence and of responsibility, man knows that Other on which he depends and to whom he is responsible in the very same act by which he knows himself. As he can never know himself save as dependent and responsible, he can never know himself without a consciousness of that Other Not-self, on whom he is dependent and to whom he is responsible; and in this co-knowledge of self and Over-not-self is rooted the whole body of his religious conceptions, religious feelings, and religious actions—which are just as inevitable functionings of his intellect, sensibility, and will as any actions of those faculties, the most intimate and immediate we can conceive of. Thus man cannot help being religious; God is implicated in his very first act of self-consciousness, and he can avoid thinking of God, feeling toward Him, acting with respect to Him, only by avoiding thinking, feeling, and acting with respect to self.

How he shall conceive God—what notion he shall form, that is, of that Over-not-self in contrast with which he is conscious of dependence and responsibilty; how he shall feel toward God —that is, toward that Over-not-self, conceived after this fashion or that; how he shall comport himself toward God—that is, over against that Over-not-self, so and not otherwise conceived, and so and not otherwise felt toward: these questions, it is obvious, raise additional problems, the solution of which must wait upon accurate knowledge of the whole body of conditions and circumstances in which the faculties of intellect, feeling, and will function in each given case. But that in his very first act of consciousness of self as a dependent and responsible and not as a self-centered and self-sufficient being, man is brought into contact with the Over-not-self on which he is dependent and to which he is responsible; and must therefore form some conception of it, feel in some way toward it, and act in some manner with respect to it, is as certain as that he will think and feel and act at all.

That man is a religious being, therefore, and will certainly have a religion, is rooted in his very nature, and is as inevitable as it is that man will everywhere and always be man. But what religion man will have is no more subject to exact *a priori* determination than is the product of the action of his faculties along any other line of their functioning. Religion exists and must exist everywhere where man lives and thinks and feels and acts; but the religions that exist will be as varied as the idiosyncrasies of men, the conditions in which their faculties work, the influences that play on them and determine the character of their thoughts and feelings and deeds.

Bearing this in mind, we shall not be surprised to note that along with the recognition of the religiousness of man embodied in the apostolic teaching, there is equally prominent in it, as we have said, the unwavering assertion of the absolute necessity of religious instruction for the proper religious development of man.

The whole mission of the apostle is founded upon, or, more properly speaking, is the appropriate expression of, this point of sight. Nor could he be untrue to it on an occasion like that which is more particularly engaging our attention to-day. We observe, then, as we have already pointed out, that though he commends the Athenians for their God-fearingness and finds in their altar to a "not-known god" a point of attachment for his proclamation of the true God; he does not for a moment suggest that their native religiousness could be left safely to itself to blossom into a fitting religious life; or that his proclamation of the known God of heaven and earth possessed only a relative necessity for them.

Clearly he presents the necessity rather as absolute. God had for a time, no doubt, left the nations of the world to the guidance of their own religious nature, that they might seek after Him in the possible expectation at least of finding Him. But on God's part this was intended rather as a demonstration of their incapacity than as a hopeful opportunity afforded them; and in its results it provides an empirical proof of the absolute necessity of His interference with direct guidance.

Accordingly the apostle roundly characterizes the issue of all heathen religious development, inclusive of that in Athens itself, the seat of the highest heathen thinking on divine things, as just bald ignorance. That the world by its wisdom knows not God and lies perishing in its ignorance is the most fixed element of his whole religious philosophy.

What is involved here is, of course, the whole question of the necessity of "special revelation." It is a question which has been repeatedly fought out during the course of Christian history. In the eighteenth century, for example, it was this very issue that was raised in the sharpest possible form by the deistic controversy. A coterie of religious philosophers, possessing an eye for little in man beyond his logical understanding, undertook to formulate what they called the "natural religion." This they then set over against the supernatural religion, which Christianity professed to be, as the religion of nature in contrast with the religion of authority—authority being prejudged to be in this sphere altogether illegitimate. The result was certainly instructive. Bernard Pünger is not a jot too severe when he remarks of this boasted "natural religion" of the Deists, that it deserves neither element of its designation. "It is," he declares, "neither religion nor natural, but only an extremely artificial abstraction of theologians and philosophers. It is no religion, for nowhere, in no spot, in either the old or new world, has there ever existed even the smallest community which recognized this 'natural religion.' And it is not natural; for no simple man ever arrived of himself at the ideas of this 'natural religion.'"

And when it was thus at last formulated by the philosophers of the eighteenth century, it proved no religion even to them. A meager body of primary abstract truth concerning God and His necessary relations to man was the entire result. This formed, indeed, an admirable witness to the rational rooting of these special truths concerning God and our relations to Him in the very nature of man as a dependent and responsible being; and this the Christian thinker may well view with satisfaction. It may be taken as supplying him also with a demonstration, once for all, that an adequate body of religious truth can never be obtained by the artificial process of abstracting from all the religions of the world the elements held in common by them all, and labeling this "natural religion." Neither in religion nor in any other sphere of life can the maxim be safely adopted that the least well-endowed member of a coterie shall be crowned king over all. Yet obviously that is the result of proceeding by what is called "the consensus method" in seeking a norm of religious truth.

Taught wisdom by experience like this, our more modern world has found a new method of ridding itself of the necessity of revelation. The way was pointed out to it by no less a genius than Friedrich Schleiermacher himself. Led no doubt by the laudable motive of seeking a place for religion unassailable on the shallow ground of intellectualistic criticism, he relegated it in its origin exclusively to the region of feeling. In essence he said, religion is the immediate feeling of absolute dependence.

He calls it an "immediate feeling" or an "immediate self-consciousness" just in order to eliminate from it every intellectual element. That is to say, he wishes to distinguish between two forms of self-consciousness or feeling, the one mediated by the perception of an object and the other not so mediated, but consisting in an immediate and direct sensation, abstracted from every intellectual representation or idea; and in this latter class of feelings he places that feeling of absolute dependence with which he identifies religion. Religion, therefore, it is argued, is entirely independent of every intellectual conception; it is rooted in a pure feeling or immediate consciousness which enters into and affects all of our intellectual exercises, but is itself absolutely independent of them all, and persists the same through whatever intellectual conceptions we may form of the object of our worship or through whatever actions we may judge appropriate to the service of that object thus or otherwise conceived.

Upon the basis of this mode of conceiving religion we have been treated of late to innumerable pæans to religion as a primal force running through all the religions; and are being constantly exhorted to recognize as absolutely immaterial what forms it takes in its several manifestations, and to greet it as subsisting equally valid and equally noble beneath all its forms of manifestation indifferently, because in itself independent of them all. It is thus only the common cry that echoes all around us which Père Hyacinthe repeats in his passionate declaration: "It is not true that all religions are false except one only."

Only a few years ago when a professor was being inducted into a new chair of the History of Religion established in one of the oldest of the Reformed schools, he took up the same cry with much the same passion, and professed himself able to feel brotherhood with every form of religion—except that perhaps which arrogated to itself to be the only legitimate form. "When the history of religions," he eloquently said, "places in our hands the religious archives of humanity it is surely our duty rather to garner these treasures than to proclaim Christianity the only good, the only true one among the religions of men. 'We also, we also are the offspring of God,' the poet Aratus cried three centuries before Christ. Let us pause before this cry of the human soul and let us contemplate with attention the luminous web in which the history of this divine sonship has been woven by universal worship. When we have opened, with the same respect which we demand for our own, the sacred books of other peoples, when we have observed them clinging, as to their most holy possessions, to their sublime traditions, in which are enshrined the mother-thoughts of all true religion—lavishing their genius in exalting them, sacrificing their fortunes in defending them, exiling themselves to the most distant lands and sinking into the burning sands in propagating them, accepting death itself in order to preserve them—our hearts, moved with surprise and brotherly

FALSE RELIGIONS AND THE TRUE

sympathy, will repudiate for ever the Pharisaic pride which treats as heathen or as uncircumcised all God's creatures which are without the sacred pale of the elect." " Men of all nations," he tells us, " and of all tongues—whether savage or civilized, whether ignorant or instructed, whether Parsi or Christian—though God may have been revealed to them diversely, though they may be looking up to Him through variously-colored glasses—are yet all looking nevertheless up to the same God, by whatever liturgical name He may be known to them—and it is to Him that all their prayers alike are ascending. And to all of them," he adds, " I feel myself a brother—except to the hypocrite." " No one," he concludes, " who has ever felt echoing in his heart the murmur of this universal worship will ever be able to return to the sectarian apologetics with which the unhappiness of the times inspired the Jews after the exile, and which from Judaism has passed into the Church of Christ."

I have not thus adverted to this eloquent address because it is especially extreme in its assertions. It is not. Rather, let it be said, it enunciates with unusual balance and moderation views common to a large part of the modern world. It is on this very account that I have adduced its presentation of this very widespread conception—because it affords us a very favorable opportunity to observe it at its best, touched with fervor and announced with winning eloquence of speech. Even in it, however, we may perceive the portentous results to which the whole conception of religion as an "immediate feeling" may take us—nay, must inevitably carry us. If what it tells us be true, it obviously is of no importance whatever with what conceptions religion may be connected. So only the religious sentiment be present, all that enters into the essence of religion is there; and one may call himself Brahmin or Mohammedan, Parsi or Christian, and may see God through whatever spectacles and name Him by whatever designation he will, and yet be and remain alike, and alike, validly, religious. We may justly look upon this inevitable result of the identification of religion with an "immediate feeling" as its sufficient refutation.

In no event could it be thought difficult, however, to exhibit the untenability of this entire conception. We should probably only need to ask, How could an abstract feeling of dependence, with no implication whatever of the object on which the dependence leans, possess any distinctively religious quality whatever? It would appear too clear to require arguing that the whole religious quality of a feeling of dependence, recognized as religious, must be derived necessarily from the nature of the object depended upon—viz., God. If we conceive that object as something other than God, then the feeling of dependence ceases to be in any intelligible sense religious. It is assuredly only on God that a specifically religious feeling can rest.

Schleiermacher himself appears to have felt this. And accordingly he distinguished between the feeling of dependence in general and the feeling of absolute dependence in particular; and on the supposition that absolute dependence can be felt only toward the Absolute, confined the religious feeling to it. Here there appears to be a subintroduction of the idea of God; and therefore a veiled admission that we have in this "feeling of absolute dependence" not an "immediate feeling," but a feeling mediated by an idea, to wit, the idea of God. Thus the whole contention is, in principle, yielded; and we revert to the more natural and only valid ground—that all their quality is supplied to feelings by the objects to which they are directed, and that, therefore, the nature of our conceptions so far from having nothing, has everything, to do with religion.

I recall with great vividness of memory a striking picture I once saw, painted by that weird Russo-German genius Sasha Schneider, in order to illustrate religion conceived as the feeling of absolute dependence, and at the same time to express the artist's repugnance to it and scorn of it. It has seemed to me to provide us with a most striking parable. He figures a man stripped naked and laden down with chains, head bowed, in every trait dejection, every fiber of every muscle relaxed, every line a line of hopelessness and despair. The ground on which he stands is the earth itself, fashioned, however, into the hideous presentment of a monstrous form, so painted as to give it the texture of hard, black, iron-like stone. The horizon that stretches around the figure and seems to bend in upon him consists of two great iron-like arms ending in dreadfully protuberant fingers, which appear about to close in on his limbs; while just before him heavy shoulders rise slightly into a low forbidding hillock, and between them thrusts forward the hard mound of a scarce-distinguishable head, lit by two malevolent eyes, like low volcano-fires glaring up upon their victim. Thus is set forth the artist's conception of religious sentiment as the "feeling of absolute dependence."

Yes—but we then must add, there are two points that require criticism in the conception presented. First, in this figure of a despondent man, the artist has, after all, painted not the feeling of dependence, but rather the feeling of helplessness. These are very different things. And in their difference we touch, as I think, the very heart of the error we are seeking to unmask. A feeling of dependence, properly so-called, necessarily implies an object: helplessness—yes, that may exist without an object, but not dependence. He that depends must needs have somewhat on which to depend. A feeling of dependence is unthinkable apart from the object on which the dependence rests. In picturing for us abject "helplessness," then, the artist has not at all pictured for us "dependence." The former is passive, the latter is active, and the abjectness that belongs to the one is not at all inherent in the other. Secondly, even so, the artist has not been able to get along without an object. He has painted this dejected man: there he stands before us the very picture of helplessness. But the artistic sense is not satisfied: and so he throws around him these hideous encircling arms; he sets upon him this baleful gaze. He must suggest, after all, an object toward which the feeling of dependence he is endeavoring to depict turns. But why this hideous object? Only to justify the abjectness of the figure he has painted. From which we may learn at once that the character of the feeling—all that gives quality and meaning to it—is, after all, necessarily dependent on the nature of the object to which it is referred.

And so, if we mistake not, Sasha Schneider's picture is itself the sufficient refutation of the whole conception of religion we are discussing. Given no object, the figure of helplessness remains inexplicable and meaningless and will result in nothing. Given a monstrous object, it develops at once into a figure of abject misery. Given a glorious object—a God of righteousness and goodness—and only then does it develop into a figure of that dependence which we call religion. And if we require an earthly image of this feeling of dependence, let us find it in an infant on its mother's bosom, looking up in confidence and trust into a face on which it perceives the smiles of goodness and love. Even the heathen poet tells us that the happy infant laughs as it sees the smile of love on the mother's countenance. It is in such scenes as this that the true earthly portrait of the absolute dependence, which is religion is to be found.

But it is neither to logical analysis nor to the artistic instinct of a Sasha Schneider that we need to turn to-day to assure ourselves that this whole construction of religion as independent of knowledge is impossible. For surely it is obvious that it is the very antipodes of Paul's view of the matter. This we have already sufficiently pointed out, and need only now to remind ourselves of it.

Perhaps it is enough for this purpose simply to ask afresh how Paul dealt with the religiousness of the Athenians, notable as they were among all nations for their religiousness. Assuredly he did not withhold due recognition from it. "O men of Athens," he cried, "I perceive that in all things ye are exceedingly religious." But did he account this exceeding religiousness enough for their needs? As he went about the streets of Athens and beheld the great city studded with idols—one great sanctuary, as it were—did he reason within himself that the forms of manifestation were of no importance, that through and beneath them we should rather perceive that pure impulse to worship which sustained and gave vitality and value to them all; and, observing in it the essence of all religions alike, recognize it as enough?

Our text gives us the emphatic answer: "What ye, thus, in ignorance adore, that it is that I declare unto you." The whole justification of his mission hangs on the value he attaches to knowledge as the informing principle of all right, of all valid, of all availing religion. And if we care to follow Paul we must for our part also, once and for all, renounce with the strongest emphasis all attempts to conceive the native religious impulse as capable in sinful man of producing religious phenomena which can be recognized as well pleasing in the sight of God.

No doubt we shall be under manifold temptations to do otherwise. Our modern atmosphere is charged to saturation with temptations to do otherwise. Let us all the more carefully arm ourselves against them. In warning us against this overestimate of natural religions Paul may perhaps be allowed to give us also a name for it, by the employment of which we may possibly be able to put a new point on our self-admonitions. He calls it, as we have seen, in the case of the Athenians, by a term of somewhat peculiar flavor. "Divinity-fearing" we bunglingly translate it—

that is, so to say, "generally Divinity-fearing," without too close inquisition into which divinity it is that we fear or what is the character of the service that we render it. "Deisidaimonism" is the Greek term he makes use of. It is an uncouth term. But, then, it is not a very lovely thing it designates. And perhaps, in the absence of a good translation, we may profitably adopt the Greek term to-day, with all its uncouthness of sound and its unlovely association, and so enable ourselves to make a recognizable distinction between that general natural religiosity and its fruits which we may call "deisidaimonism" and true religion, which is the product of the saving truth of God operating upon our native religious instincts and producing through them phenomena which owe all their value to the truth that gives them form.

Ah, brethren, let us avoid "deisidaimonism" in all its manifestations! As you look out over the heathen world with its lords many and gods many, and see working in every form of faith the same religious impulses, the same religious aspirations, producing in varying measure indeed, but yet everywhere, to some extent, the same civilizing and moralizing effects—are you perhaps sometimes tempted to pronounce it enough; possibly adding something about the special adaptation of the several faiths to the several peoples, or even something about the essential truth underlying all religions? This is "deisidaimonism." And on its basis the whole missionary work of the Church is an impertinence, the whole history of the Church a gigantic error; the great commission itself a crime against humanity—launching the Christian world upon a fool's errand, every step of which has dripped with wasted blood. Surely the proclamation of the gospel is made, then, mere folly and the blood of the martyrs becomes only the measure of the narrow fanaticism of earlier and less enlightened times.

It is possible, however, that your temptation does not come to you in such a crass shape. Perhaps it may whisper to you only something about the narrowness of sectarianism within the limits of Christianity—of the folly of contentions over what we may at the moment be happening to call "the truth." Look, it may say—do you not see that under every faith the religious life flourishes? Why lay stress then on creed? Creeds are divisive things; away with them! Or at least let us prune all their distinctive features away, and give ourselves a genial and unpolemic Christianity, a Christianity in which all the stress is laid on life, not dogma, the life of the spirit in its aspirations toward God, or perchance, even the life of external activities in the busy fulfillment of the duties of life. This too, you observe, is "deisidaimonism." Embark once on that pathway and there is no logical and—oh, the misfortune of it!—no practical stopping-point until you have evaporated all recognizable Christianity away altogether and reduced all religion to the level of man's natural religiosity. A really "undogmatic Christianity" is just no Christianity at all.

Let us not for an instant suppose, to be sure, that religion is a matter of the intellect alone or chiefly. But in avoiding the Scylla of intellectualism let us not run into the Charybdis of mere naturalism. All that makes the religion we profess distinctively Christian is enshrined in its doctrinal system. It is therefore that it is a religion that can be taught, and is to be taught—that is propagated by what otherwise would be surely, in the most literal sense, the foolishness of preaching. Mere knowledge, indeed, does not edify; it only puffs up. But neither without knowledge can there be any edification; and the purer the knowledge that is propagated by any church the purer, the deeper, the more vital and the more vitalizing will be the Christianity that is built up under that church's teaching. Let us renounce, then, in this sphere, too, all "deisidaimonism," and demand that our church shall be the church of a creed and that that creed shall be the pure truth of God—all of it and nothing but it. Only so can we be truly, purely, and vitally Christian.

And what shall we say of "deisidaimonism" in the personal religious life? Ah, brethren, there is where its temptations are the most subtle and its assaults the most destructive! How easy it is to mistake the currents of mere natural religious feeling, that flow up and down in the soul, for signs that it is well with us in the sight of God! Happy the man who is born with a deep and sensitive religious nature! But shall that purely natural endowment save him? There are many who have cried, Lord, Lord, who shall never enter into the kingdom of heaven. Not because you are sensitive and easily moved to devotion; not because your sense of divine things is profound or lofty; not because you are like the Athenians, by nature "divinity-fearing"; but because, when the word of the Lord is brought to you, and Jesus Christ is revealed in your soul, under the prevailing influence of the Holy Ghost, you embrace Him with a hearty faith—cast yourself upon His almighty grace for salvation, and turning from your sins, enter into a life of obedience to Him—can you judge yourself a Christian. Religious you may be, and deeply religious, and yet not a Christian. How instructive that when Paul himself preached in "deisidaimonistic" Athens, where religiosity ran riot, no church seems to have been founded. We have only the meager result recorded that "there were some men that clave unto him and believed, among whom also was Dionysius, the Areopagite, and a woman named Damaris, and others along with them." The natively religious are not, therefore, nearer to the kingdom of God.

But, thank God, the contrary is also true. Those who have no special native religious endowments are not, therefore, excluded from the kingdom of God. We may rightly bewail our coldness: we may rightly blame ourselves that there is so little response in our hearts to the sight of the glory of God in the face of Jesus Christ, or even to the manifestation of His unspeakable love in the death of His Son. Oh, wretched men that we are to see that bleeding love and not be set on fire with a flame of devotion! But we may be all the more thankful that it is not in our frames and feelings that we are to put our trust. Let us abase ourselves that we so little respond to these great spectacles of the everlasting and unspeakable love of God. But let us ever remember that it is on the love of God and not on our appreciation of it that we are to build our confidence. Jesus our Priest and our Sacrifice, let us keep our eyes set on Him! And though our poor sinful hearts so little know how to yield to that great spectacle the homage of a suitable response, His blood will yet avail even for us.

> "Nothing in my hand I bring,
> Simply to Thy cross I cling"—

here—and let us bless God for it—here is the essence of Christianity. It is all of God and nothing of ourselves.

APPENDIX

Hymns and Religious Verses by B.B. Warfield

THE LOVE OF GOD ALMIGHTY.

Rev. B. F. ALLEMAN, D.D.

O the love of God Almighty, O His ceaseless love!
Piercing thro' the depths beneath us, Through the heights above;
Wider than the boundless spaces, Where the stars do dwell;
Kindling heaven with its brightness, Reaching down to hell;
Kindling heaven with its brightness, Reaching down to hell.

Yea, our mother may forget us;
Yea, our father fail;
Yea, the bridegroom may grow careless,—
Other thoughts prevail:
We may change, and all the whiteness
Of our souls may blot:
O the love of God Almighty,
Lo, it changes not.

Holy is the Lord Almighty,
Righteous past compare:
We are sinners,—who among us
Can His vengeance bear?
Lo the Cross! and One upon it
Coming from above!
O the love of God Almighty,
O His Saving love!

LORD GOD OF ALL THE AGES!

(ST. GEORGE'S, BOLTON.)

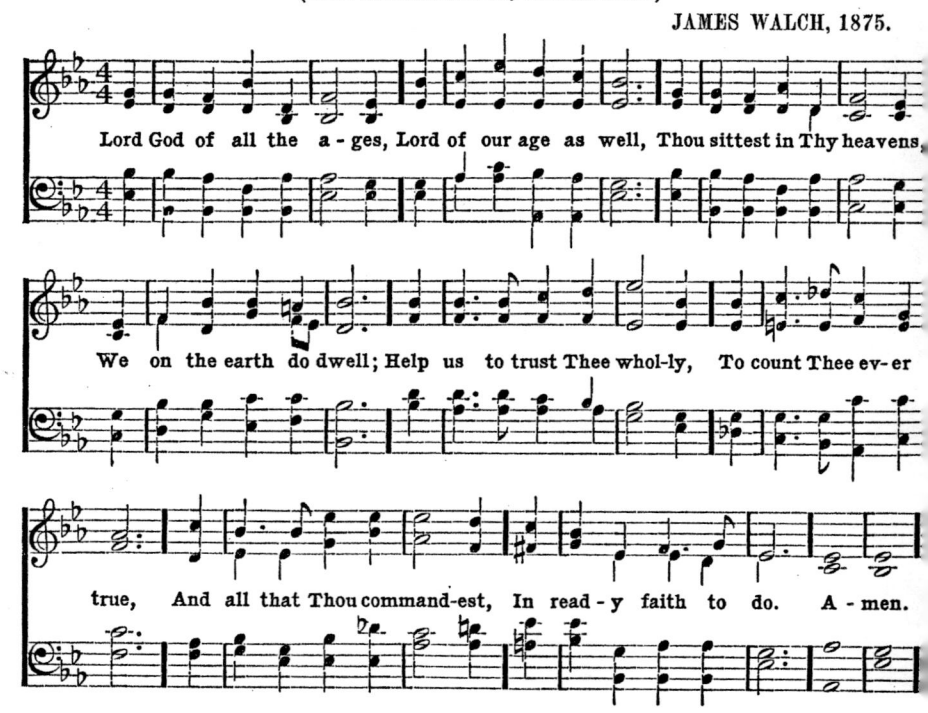

JAMES WALCH, 1875.

Lord God of all the a-ges, Lord of our age as well, Thou sittest in Thy heavens, We on the earth do dwell; Help us to trust Thee whol-ly, To count Thee ev-er true, And all that Thou command-est, In read-y faith to do. A-men.

We hear the heathen raging, the world's rebellious roar,—
Thy bands they cast off from them, Thy sceptre own no more;
Yet still Thy voice is calling to all who will but hear;
Still through the murky darkness Thy light is shining clear.

This shadow that we dwell in, it too shall pass away,
As more and more dawns on us the splendor of Thy day;
O help us in our weakness Thine empire to confess,
And fill our hearts with courage to trust Thy faithfulness.

Lord God of all the ages, the future as the past,
And of these times of evil in which our lot is cast,
Help us to hear with trembling, the while our hearts rejoice,
The thunders of Thy marching, the whispers of Thy voice.

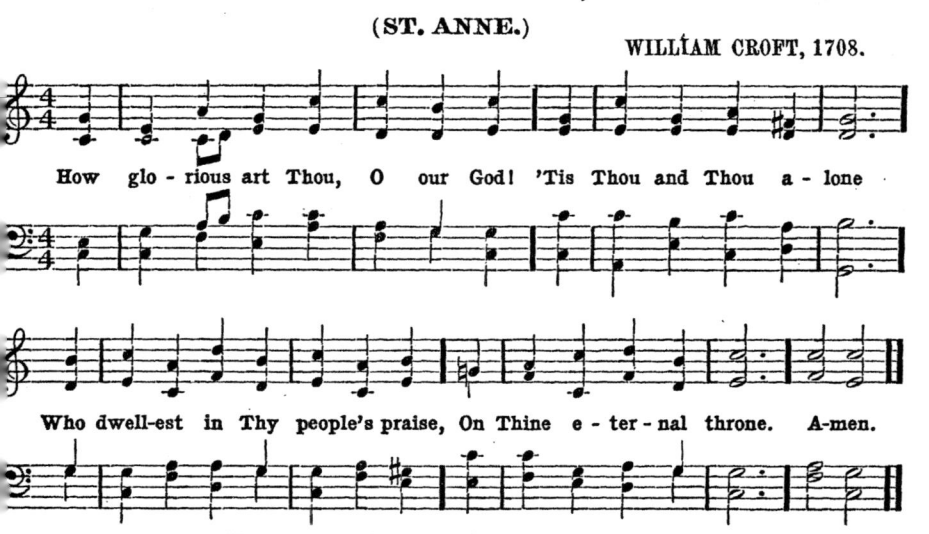

HOW GLORIOUS ART THOU, O OUR GOD!
(ST. ANNE.)
WILLIAM CROFT, 1708.

How glorious art Thou, O our God! 'Tis Thou and Thou alone
Who dwellest in Thy people's praise, On Thine eternal throne. Amen.

How many voices, diff'ring tongues,
  Harmonious, join to raise
To Thee, O Rock of Israel,
  Accumulating praise!

From Charran and Chaldean Ur,
  The River's banks along,
From Canaan's heights and Egypt's sands,
  Ascends the constant song,—

From all the towns that stud the hills
  Of teeming Galilee,
From marts of Greece and misty lands
  Beyond the Western Sea.

Fain would we catch the accents strange,
  Fain train our ears to hear
The notes that hymn Thee through the years,
  O Israel's Hope and Fear!

'Twas Thou didst teach Thy Sons of old
  Thy varied laud to sing,
School Thou our hearts that we may too
  Our hallelujahs bring.

How glorious art Thou, O our God!
  How mighty past compare!
Thou dwellest in Thy people's praise,—
  Accept the praise we bear.

HYMN FOR THE OPENING OF THE SEMINARY.

(SARUM.)

Sir JOSEPH BARNBY, 1869.

Great God the Giv-er, Thou hast faith-ful been, Here Thou hast set Thy name, and we have seen Thy mer-cies grow from year to year more green,—Lord, we thank Thee, Lord, we thank Thee. A-men.

'Twas Thou didst raise these walls: and Thou didst give
Thy saints Thy truth to teach, Thy truth to live;
They wrought their work, and Thou didst it receive,—
    Lord, we thank Thee.

Unto their feet Thou gatheredst of Thy Sons,—
The love of Thee waxed fire within their bones,
The world has heard their voice,—its huts, its thrones,—
    Lord, we thank Thee.

God of our fathers, still pour out Thy grace
In plenteous streams upon this hallowed place,
Still show it all Thy glorious faithfulness,
    Lord, we pray Thee.

And as the flood of years rolls ever by,
Build here Thy holy house each year more high,
Establish here Thy truth unchangeably,—
    Lord, we pray Thee.

And every year send forth a sacred host,
Taught of thy Christ, filled with the Holy Ghost,
The cross their only theme, their only boast,
    Lord, we pray Thee.

The Advent

The Lord has come into His world!
    "Nay, nay, that cannot be:
The world is full of noisomeness
    And all iniquity;
The Lord—thrice holy is His name—
He cannot touch this thing of shame."

The Lord has come into His world!
    "Ah, then, He comes in might,
The sword of fury in His hands,
    With vengeance all bedight!
O wretched world! Thine end draws near,
Prepare to meet thy God, in fear!"

The Lord has come into His world!
    "What! In that baby sweet?
That broken man, acquaint with grief?
    Those bleeding hands and feet?
He is the Lord of all the earth,
How can He stoop to human birth?"

The Lord has come into His world!
    "A slaughtered Lamb I see,
A smoking altar, on which burns
    A sacrifice for me!
He comes—He comes—O blessed day!—
He comes to take my sin away!"

The Mower

A MOWER went forth to mow,
    And crooned his workman's song:—
"Swing, swing, O mower, thy goodly scythe,
    Make the swath both wide and long."

Gaily the grasses grow,
    And fling their heads in pride:—
"Swing, swing, O mower, thy goodly scythe,
    Make the swath both long and wide."

Quiet they lie behind,
    Each by his neighbor's side:—
"Swing, swing, O mower, thy goodly scythe,
    Make the swath both long and wide."

Though every spear of them all
    Be a man in right or in wrong:—
"Swing, swing, O mower, thy goodly scythe,
    Make the swath both wide and long."

Augustine's Philosophy

"There is a place for everything,
    In earth or sky or sea,
Where it may find its proper use
    And of advantage be,"
        Quoth Augustine, the saint.

The mocker quick, with curling lip: —
    "Then there's a place for vice!"
"Yea, fitly 'neath our trampling feet,
    May lie the cockatrice,"
        Quoth Augustine, the saint.

"Our very vices, great and foul,
    When in the earth they're trod,
May haply lofty ladders build
    On which to climb to God,"
        Quoth Augustine, the saint.

Prayer and Work

Said one, one day: "My cause is good,
    The Lord will prosper it."
Said Luther, "Take it to Him, then;
    That were provision fit.

"Trust in the Lord, not in thy cause,
    However good it be;
Take it forthwith in faithful hands
    And lay it on His knee.

"The best of causes go amiss;
    The Lord will never fail:
Commit thy ways into His care,
    And then—shake out thy sail."

Wanted — A Samaritan

Prone in the road he lay,
        Wounded and sore bested;
Priests, Levites, passed that way,
        And turned aside the head.

They were not hardened men
        In human service slack:
His need was great: but then,
        His face, you see, was black.

Trusting in the Dark

Said Robert Leighton, holy man,
    Intent a flickering faith to fan
    Into a steady blaze:—
"Behold yon floweret to the sun,
As he his daily course doth run,
    Turn undeclining gaze.

"E'en when the clouds obscure his face,
And only faith discerns the place
    Where in the heavens he soars,
This floweret still, with constant eye,
The secret places of the sky
    Untiringly explores.

"Look up, my soul! What can this be
But Nature's parable to thee?
    Look up, with courage bright!
The clouds press on thee, dense and black,
Thy Sun shines ever at their back—
    Look up and see His light!"

The Blood of the Lamb

I dreamed a dream on yesternight:—
A charnel house rose on my sight,
Vast, crowded, horrible. Untold
In numbers, in the gathered mould
Of untold numbers more, the dead
Lay heaped, each frame, each ghastly head
Oozing corruption. Suddenly
A great voice sounded, crying, See!
And lo! a Lamb amid these dead,
With wounded feet and wounded head,
And wounded side, wherefrom the blood
Surged in a never-ceasing flood.
Again the voice cried, See! And lo!
The Lamb was moving on with slow
Calm steps, the serried ranks to thread;
And, passing, lo! There were no dead,
But in their place a gathering train
Hymning the Lamb which had been slain.

In the Theatre — Third Century

"Yes, Rome hath many mimes of skill, but yet
    But one Genesius. For who but he
    Hath power to make us roar with frantic glee
The while, in Galilean wise, all wet
With 'sacred water,' sore with blows and th' fret
    Of chains well-merited, he skulks . . . But see!
    He comes! Hear how they greet him! Note how free,
How sure his play! The very thing! I'll get
The cramps from laughter! . . . Bah! What ails him now?
    The baptizing scene's his best, — and there all white
He stands, and trembling! Ill? Nay, what says he?
'A Christian! Christ the Lord hath set him free!'
To the lions with the booby! . . . Yet, somehow,
    I doubt . . . What makes the fellow's face so bright?"

In the World — Twentieth Century

Genesius on the stage of Rome, what time
    The heathens' rage imagined vanity,
    Made sport of Christ, until the all-seeing eye
Observed and pitied the deluded mime.
At once the scales fell from him; and sublime
    In holy courage, as his blasphemy
    E'en so his faith he published openly, —
Wherefor he died before the winter's rime.

Dear Lord, how oft do we on narrower stage
    Like him deny Thee, if but we may win
        Applauding smiles from those who love Thee not?
    O grant us too to hate the world's mad din,
        That clamors 'gainst Thee, and, our shame forgot,
On heart and lips to bear Thy name from age to age.

Out of the Night-Watches

Peace! Peace! The night will pass! No, no, not yet
      The robin's call awakes the drowsy day.
      Nay, 'tis the robin! And from far away
An oriole's whistle! How the sparrows fret,
A noisier Babel in my hedge-row set;
      They quarrel with the dawn! And hark, that bay
      Of dog! And now a footfall on the way!
'Tis morning beating at my lattice-net!

Great God, the light is Thine: nay, Thou art light!
      O that this restless longing of my heart
          Might pipe me warning of Thy rising rays!
So would my fretting thoughts of yesternight
      Cease their complaining, and employ their art
          To drown the darkness in their iterant praise.

Apocalyptics

In His own time, in His own way, He came,
      The Hope of Israel: not in such guise
      As flared before the anger-smarting eyes
Of those old watchers, who, in stolen name
Of seer or sibyl (heedless of their shame),
      Would drown in glory present infamies,—
      Prophets of hope, but prophets too of lies,
With vengeful passion, not with love, aflame.
God's ways are not as ours: the sun shall cease
      Before His glory when He comes again;
      As when He came at first, all thoughts of men,
Their dreams of unfound joys, of untried peace,
Their hopes of succor in their bitter ruth,
Stood all abashed before the unimagined truth.

Other SGCB Classic Reprints

In addition to *The Power of God unto Salvation* which you now hold in your hands, Solid Ground Christian Books is honored to present the following titles, many for the first time in more than a century:

THEOLOGY ON FIRE: *Sermons from the Heart of J.A. Alexander*
A SHEPHERD'S HEART: *Sermons from the Ministry of J.W. Alexander*
A GENTLEMAN & A SCHOLAR: *Memoir of James P. Boyce by John Albert Broadus*
OPENING SCRIPTURE: *A Hermeneutical Manual by Patrick Fairbairn*
THE ASSURANCE OF FAITH *by Louis Berkhof*
THE PASTOR IN THE SICK ROOM *by John D. Wells*
THE NATIONAL PREACHER: *Sermons from the 2nd Great Awakening*
THE POOR MAN'S OT COMMENTARY *by Robert Hawker* (6 vols)
THE POOR MAN'S NT COMMENTARY *by Robert Hawker* (3 vols)
FIRST THINGS: *The First Lessons God Taught Mankind by Gardiner Spring*
BIBLICAL & THEOLOGICAL STUDIES *by the 1912 Faculty of Princeton*
EVANGELICAL TRUTH *by Archibald Alexander*
THE LORD OF GLORY *by B.B. Warfield*
CHRIST ON THE CROSS & THE LORD OUR SHEPHERD *by John Stevenson*
SERMONS TO THE NATURAL MAN *by W.G.T. Shedd*
SERMONS TO THE SPIRITUAL MAN *by W.G.T. Shedd*
HOMILETICS AND PASTORAL THEOLOGY *by W.G.T. Shedd*
A PASTOR'S SKETCHES 1 & 2 *by Ichabod S. Spencer*
THE PREACHER AND HIS MODELS *by James Stalker*
IMAGO CHRISTI *by James Stalker*
A HISTORY OF PREACHING *by Edwin C. Dargan*
LECTURES ON THE HISTORY OF PREACHING *by John A. Broadus*
THE SCOTTISH PULPIT *by William Taylor*
THE SHORTER CATECHISM ILLUSTRATED *by John Whitecross*
THE CHURCH MEMBER'S GUIDE *by John Angell James*
THE SUNDAY SCHOOL TEACHER'S GUIDE *by John Angell James*
CHRIST IN SONG: *Hymns of Immanuel from All Ages by Philip Schaff*
COME YE APART: *Daily Words from the Four Gospels by J.R. Miller*
DEVOTIONAL LIFE OF THE SUNDAY SCHOOL TEACHER *by J.R. Miller*

Call us Toll Free at 1-877-666-9469
Send us an e-mail at sgcb@charter.net
Visit us on line at solid-ground-books.com

"Uncovering Buried Treasure to the Glory of God"

Printed in the United States
40852LVS00002B/60